Elizabeth Wallace

The Constitution of the Argentine Republic

The constitution of the United States of Brazil, with historical introduction

and notes

Elizabeth Wallace

The Constitution of the Argentine Republic
The constitution of the United States of Brazil, with historical introduction and notes

ISBN/EAN: 9783337384104

Printed in Europe, USA, Canada, Australia, Japan

Cover: Foto ©ninafisch / pixelio.de

More available books at **www.hansebooks.com**

The University of Chicago
DEPARTMENT OF POLITICAL SCIENCE

THE CONSTITUTION
OF THE
ARGENTINE REPUBLIC

THE CONSTITUTION
OF THE
UNITED STATES OF BRAZIL

WITH HISTORICAL INTRODUCTION AND NOTES

BY

ELIZABETH WALLACE
DOCENT IN SPANISH AND IN LATIN-AMERICAN

THE CONSTITUTION OF THE ARGENTINE REPUBLIC

THE CONSTITUTION OF THE UNITED STATES OF BRAZIL

WITH HISTORICAL INTRODUCTION AND NOTES

BY

ELIZABETH WALLACE

DOCENT IN SPANISH AND IN LATIN-AMERICAN INSTITUTIONS

CHICAGO
The University Press of Chicago
1894

PRINTED AT
The University Press of **Chicago.**
D. C. HEATH & CO., Directors.

Part I.

THE CONSTITUTION
OF THE
ARGENTINE REPUBLIC

NOTE.

The text of the Argentine Constitution is a translation by the editor from the Spanish text issued by the Bureau of American Republics.

I.

HISTORICAL INTRODUCTION.

The territory which to-day comprises the Argentine Republic, Uruguay, Paraguay and Bolivia, originally belonged to the powerful vice-royalty of Peru, although, with the exception of Bolivia, it bore very little resemblance to Peru proper. The lands watered by the Paraná and La Plata were thinly populated by Indians belonging to the Aucan tribes, a race savage and hard to civilize, while the Quichua Indians of Upper and Lower Peru were docile and had already submitted to a completely organized government.

The colonization of the two regions was also widely different. In Peru Spanish rule was substituted for the government of the Incas by means of violence, perfidy, and cruel rapacity. In the regions watered by the great rivers small groups of adventurers, widely scattered over a vast territory, carried on constant warfare with the natives and subdued them with difficulty. The occupation of these early settlers was cattle raising, the broad and fertile pampas offering them ample opportunities for this industry. The herdsmen gathered together in groups and thus formed the nucleus of towns, which, from the nature of their inhabitants, were far apart with wide stretches of country between, and were the foundation of future independent provinces. Another strong and formative influence was the fact that the Portuguese of Brazil early showed a desire to invade the territories of Uruguay and Paraguay and possess themselves of the fertile lands bordering on the River Plate, and the necessity of self-defense fostered in the Spaniards the spirit of independence. These three considerations, the character of the original inhabitants, the chief occupation of the colonists, and the necessity of self-defense and self-government, must not be lost sight of in studying the political history of these countries.

The constant warfare with the Brazilian Portuguese, and the great distance of the center of government at Lima from the seat of war, led Spain in 1776 to erect the new vice-royalty of Buenos Ayres. The capital was fixed at Buenos Ayres, and the territory embraced Uruguay and Paraguay. In 1810 the revolution broke out, precipitated by the French invasion of Spain, which was to bring about the entire independence of Spanish America. On the 25th of May, 1811, the Viceroy Cisneros assembled in the city of Buenos Ayres a Junta of nine persons endowed with full powers. Their first act was to exclude certain individuals from the government, among whom was Cisneros himself. They also resolved to unite the provinces in a congress, and for this purpose they sent out circular letters to the cities ordering deputies to be elected who should have a voice in the government. The Junta thus augmented authorized the formation in each province of Juntas of five members each, who should exercise supreme authority in that province. Jealousies soon arose in the loosely organized government of the Junta. The two leading spirits, Moreno, the President of the Junta, and General Saavedra, formed factions, which, under the names of "Morenistas" and "Saavedristas," were the germs of the future political parties, the Federalists and Unitarians. We may remark here, that the ideas which animated these two parties bore a marked resemblance to the underlying principles characterizing the two great parties which had been evolved in the growth of our own government. The Unitarian party, like the Hamiltonian Federalists, saw all the evils of provincial organization and none of the good; they wished to centralize power and form a harmonious whole. Now, all this was very good, but the one flaw was that they wanted to centralize power in Buenos Ayres and make that province the leader of the rest. On the other hand, the Federalists, like the Jeffersonian Republicans, wished to erect the provinces into sovereign and independent states, and to organize a common government only for taking measures of general defense and for conducting foreign affairs.

On October 9 of this same year, 1811, the deputies were

excluded from a share in the government, and the Junta determined to create an executive power, reserving to itself certain powers of legislation, such as providing for exigencies, restraining the operation of laws prejudicial to the state, and deliberating upon important national affairs. With these limitations the executive power was vested in a triumvirate. On the 12th of October the deputies promulgated a sort of constitution under the name of "Ordinance of the Conservative Junta, under the authority of Don Ferdinand the VII.," in which they vested in themselves the legislative power. The triumvirate disapproved of it, dissolved the Junta and tried its own hand at constitution making. On the 22d of November it published a "Provisional Law for the government of the United Provinces of the River Plate." In April, 1812, the executive power ordained that an assembly should be organized to meet at stated periods, for sessions limited strictly to eight days. This assembly should deliberate upon state affairs, and should select every six months a successor to the executive power. In accordance with this action a congress assembled in December of 1813, and owing to the warring of factions incident to a triumvirate, they elected a single executive, Don Jervasio Posadas. In 1814 a Junta of Observation was erected for the purpose of restraining the directorial power, and this Junta in the following year issued a "Provisional Statute," a constitution emphasizing Federal ideas.

Another congress assembled in Tucumán in March of 1816, and on the 9th of July proclaimed the independence of the country from Spanish rule. The country had been independent in fact for six years, and active hostilities had ceased in 1814. This same congress transferred to Buenos Ayres, issued in 1817 a "Provisional Ordinance" [*Reglamento Provisorio*] containing marked Unitarian ideas. Except in the case of the election of cabildos the whole was merely a reorganization of the colonial vice-royalty.

In 1819 a constitution was framed which satisfied no one, for it compromised none of the disputes which divided the two parties and contained no regulations concerning the local government of the provinces. From 1820 to 1825 the provinces had no common government, but by independent acts conducted their own affairs. It was a time when provincial chiefs grew into tyrants, and when gauchos became improvised statesmen. Only in Buenos Ayres from 1821 to 1827 was there a government with any degree of stability. This province assumed some of the most indispensable functions of national government, basing its right on the fact that it had made treaties with foreign nations [France and England].

The Constituent Congress met again in 1824, and the next year issued a Fundamental Law that for a long time afterward was the only legal basis of the Argentine government. This congress also elected Rivadavia president in 1826, and in December of the same year approved of a constitution which was favored by Rivadavia, and which showed a Unitarian tendency. But according to the provisions of this last constitution and the Fundamental Law [1825], the ratification of the provinces was necessary. It was submitted to them, but the majority rejected it, and in turn petitioned for a federal constitution that should " insure to the provinces a perfect liberty, independence and equality." Rivadavia, disgusted with the sentiment of the people, resigned his office in 1827, and at the same time Congress declared the union between the provinces to be dissolved. The aim of Rivadavia's successor, Dorrego, was to bring the provinces together again. To this end he united them in a common alliance against Brazil, and gained their consent to submit affairs of general importance to a government centered at Buenos Ayres. At the close of the war with Brazil, General Lavalle returned, and heading an insurrection against Dorrego deposed him. General Rosas, who had been a favorite of the deposed President, now became the leader of the Federalists. Trouble arose with France in 1829 which caused the fall of Lavalle, and in December of the same year Rosas was elected Governor of Buenos Ayres. Very little was accomplished towards the establishment of national union during his administration. In 1831 a new defensive and offensive alliance was formed between the Atlantic provinces, and unsuccessful efforts were made to assemble a Congress which should unite the country under a federal system. Rosas' first term of office expired in December of 1832, and the Chamber of Representatives at Buenos Ayres wished to reëlect him, but he declined, and proposed instead to lead an expedition against the Indians of the southwest. This was done, no doubt, to render himself more popular in the eyes of the people, and thus he hoped to attain his ambition of wielding supreme power. The expedition lasted two years, and during his absence, in December of 1833, the legislature of Buenos Ayres formulated a constitution which provided that the province should not unite with the others except under a federative system, and that the provincial executive should not be vested with extraordinary powers. This greatly offended the Rosas party, who caused the constitution to be destroyed, and when their leader returned from his Indian wars they elected him governor. He pretended to decline the honor upon various vague pretexts which covered but thinly his real reason, the desire for unlimited power. Finally, on the 7th day of March, the assembly passed a law in which, "exercising its ordinary and extraordinary sovereignty," it appointed Rosas Governor and Captain-General for a term of five years with the whole substance of public power [*con la suma del poder publico*]. Rosas again declined, unless the plan should be submitted to the approval of the people; this was accordingly done, and in the city of Buenos Ayres alone, out of 9,320 votes cast, only four were unfavorable. For nearly twenty years, at intervals of five years, this farce of an election was kept up, the independent vote being suppressed by bribery and oppression. Thus General Rosas governed until 1852, at first deceiving the people, then terrorizing them by that tyranny which made him universally notorious.

After many fruitless attempts to overthrow the power of the tyrant, the Unitarians gained to their cause the federal governor of Entre Rios, Don Justo Urquiza. Uruguay, Brazil and the province of Corientes entered also into the conspiracy, and the result was the battle of Monte Casenos, a battle of little importance from a military point of view, but of vast political significance to the provinces of La Plata. The power of Rosas fell on the 3rd of

February, 1852, and, a fugitive, he embarked on an English ship and sailed to Europe. Urquiza was now, by his own act, "Supreme Provisional Director of the Argentine Confederation," but, unfortunately for his ambition, there was no real affinity between himself and the Unitarians. His band of followers was an improvised one, and after having gained the victory, the common reasons which had bound them together disappeared, and the party was resolved into its constituent elements, which proved antagonistic to Urquiza. The Unitarians had desired the immediate convocation of an assembly which should be elected under their influence. But Urquiza took other measures; he assembled the provincial governors at San Nicolás de los Arroyos on the 31st of May, and they prepared a constitution which provided for a general assembly to meet at Santa Fé in September, 1852, in which assembly the provinces were to have two representatives each. The Unitarians of Buenos Ayres, who were now in power, objected to the constitution of San Nicolás, and the Chamber of Representatives refused to carry out its provisions, alleging that it had not been properly submitted to their approval. Thereupon Urquiza dissolved the Chamber of Representatives, forbade the liberty of the press, and gathered about him in the capital his "true Federalists." In September he was forced to go to Santa Fé to open Congress, and the Unitarians of Buenos Ayres seized this opportunity, under the leadership of General Mitré, to affect a political change; this they succeeded in accomplishing on the night of the 11th of September, whereupon they organized a provincial Unitarian government, and the province declared itself separated from, and independent of, the other provinces.

The Congress of Santa Fé, delayed by these events, did not assemble until the 20th of November, and meanwhile civil war was being waged between Buenos Ayres and the provincial forces under Urquiza. In January of 1853 Congress instructed the Director to try pacific measures for urging Buenos Ayres to subscribe to the constitution; accordingly on the 9th of March an arrangement was made between Urquiza's agent and the government of Buenos Ayres by which that province should have an immediate representation in congress, and meanwhile the provincial legislature would deliberate longer upon the constitution. Urquiza refused to sanction this arrangement, claiming that congress had not given him sufficient power. The war was again renewed, and continued for a few weeks, until both parties were wearied and it stopped by mutual consent. Buenos Ayres remained independent and Urquiza contented himself with exercising authority over the thirteen provinces. On the 1st of May, 1853, congress sanctioned the constitution of the Argentine Confederation, and it was ratified by thirteen provinces, Buenos Ayres remaining independent until 1859. By the constitution of 1853 a national government was established for the first time by the voice of the Argentine people; by it civil rights were guaranteed, which heretofore had been granted or withheld according to the caprice of provincial governors who were bound neither by law nor by public opinion. This constitution held the provinces together until 1859, when war again broke out with Buenos Ayres. By the battle of Cepeda, on the 23rd of October, the forces of the refractory province were defeated and Buenos Ayres entered the confederation. Complete understanding was not yet established however. On the 30th of November a provincial congress assembled at Buenos Ayres to examine the Constitution of Santa Fé, amendments were proposed and presented to the federal congress, which summoned a general convention, in which the propositions were discussed and adopted. Urquiza's term of office was now over, and he was succeeded by Santiago Derqui. The Unitarians of Buenos Ayres again made trouble and pacific negotiations were delayed until General Mitré was elected governor of Buenos Ayres. He was friendly to the confederation and tried to reconcile the two factions. His efforts were successful, and on the 6th of June, 1860, a new treaty was made. The modifications proposed by Buenos Ayres were submitted to congress; the general convention assembled at Santa Fé accepted nearly all the solicited reforms, confirmed the constitution on the 25th of September, and on the 21st of the following October it was solemnly promulgated in the two capitals, Paraná and Buenos Ayres. But the belligerent spirit of Unitarians and Federalists had not yet been sufficiently calmed. Derqui in the confederation and Mitré in his province, who both desired a genuine reconciliation, became the object of distrust to their respective parties. Derqui unfortunately interfered with national forces in some local disturbances between San Juan and Cordova, and immediately his enemies in Buenos Ayres declared themselves against the government of the confederation. War was again begun. The federal congress went so far as to declare void the treaties of 1859 and 1860 and wished to treat the Buenos Ayrians as rebels. On the 17th of September, 1861, the opposing forces met at Pavon, and again the Buenos Ayrians were defeated, but only from a military point of view; the moral victory was theirs. The whole country arose in favor of General Mitré; even General Urquiza, disgusted with fruitless war, accepted the idea of a new government, and Derqui resigned his command and the directorship.

Invested with extraordinary powers by the provincial towns, General Mitré called a national congress, which met on the 25th of May, 1862. Mitré was elected president in accordance with the terms of the constitution of 1860, and the political code of that constitution was accepted without alteration.

The constitution of 1860 is the result of the amalgamation of two principles which were born with the colonization of the Argentine nation and grew with its peculiar civilization, in their very nature antagonistic, but by their union giving birth to elements which contain the promise of future strength and prosperity. These two principles, nationality and provincial sovereignty, were represented by two acts, the federal constitution of 1853, and the revolution of Buenos Ayres on the 11th of September, 1852. The union of these two principles formed the only basis that could give any strength to the constitution.

II.

OUTLINE OF CONTENTS.

PREAMBLE.

PART FIRST.

CHAPTER I.—DECLARATIONS, RIGHTS AND GUARANTEES.

ARTICLE.
1. Form of government.
2. Religion.
3. Capital of the nation.
4. National expenditures.
5. Form of government of provinces.
6. Federal interference in the provinces.
7. Relations between provinces.
8. Relations of citizens of one province to another province.
9. Custom houses.
10. Interstate duties.
11. Duties of passage.
12. Duties of passage.
13. Erection of new provinces.
14. Rights of inhabitants.
15. Prohibition of slavery.
16. Equality of citizens.
17. Protective provisions.
18. Protection from unlawful punishment, inviolability of domicile, etc.
19. Private interest and public welfare.
20. Rights of foreigners.
21. Duty of citizens to the country.
22. Sovereignty a delegated power.

23. Action in case of foreign invasion or domestic disturbance
24. Reforms in legislation; trial by jury.
25. Encouragement of immigration.
26. Interior navigation.
27. Treaties with foreign nations.
28. Unchangeability of rights and guarantees.
29. Prohibition of the granting of extraordinary powers to individuals.
30. Amendment of the constitution.
31. The supreme law of the land.
32. Freedom of the press.
33. Constitutional rights and guarantees not exclusive.
34. Federal judge cannot at the same time be provincial judge; concerning rights of residence.
35. Name of the republic.

PART SECOND—POWERS OF THE NATION.

TITLE I.—FEDERAL GOVERNMENT.

Section I.—The Legislative Power.

ARTICLE.
36. Structure of the Legislature.

CHAPTER I. — OF THE CHAMBER OF DEPUTIES.

37. Composition; basis of representation; number.
38. Provisions for the first legislature.
39. Provisions for the second legislature.
40. Qualifications of members.
41. Manner of election.
42. Term of office.
43. Vacancies.
44. Right of initiation.
45. Right of impeachment.

CHAPTER II. — OF THE SENATE.

46. Number of senators.
47. Qualifications of senators.
48. Term of office of senators.
49. President of senate.

THE ARGENTINE REPUBLIC. 15

50. Provision for absence of president.
51. Judicial power of senate.
52. Sentences in cases of impeachment.
53. Powers of the senate in case of invasion.
54. Provision for vacancies in the senate.

CHAPTER III. — PROVISIONS RELATING TO BOTH HOUSES.

55. Sessions of congress.
56. Powers of the houses regarding members, attendance, etc.
57. Sessions of the houses simultaneous.
58. Rules of procedure.
59. Oath of members.
60. Privileges of members.
61. Privileges of members.
62. Punishment of members.
63. Report of ministers to congress.
64. Incompatibility of membership with office-holding.
65. Ineligibility of ecclesiastics and provincial governors.
66. Compensation of members.

CHAPTER IV. — POWERS OF CONGRESS.

67—
  (1) Legislation concerning custom houses and import duties.
  (2) Levying of direct taxes.
  (3) Contracting of loans.
  (4) Concerning national lands.
  (5) Concerning national banks.
  (6) Concerning the national debt.
  (7) Concerning the national expenditures.
  (8) Granting sums to the provinces.
  (9) Regulating river navigation; suppressing provincial custom houses.
  (10) Coining of money, etc.
  (11) Dictating various codes, establishing trial by jury.
  (12) Regulating commerce.
  (13) Regulating and establishing postoffices and postroads.
  (14) Fixing territorial limits.

(15) Regarding Indians.
(16) Concerning general good of the nation.
(17) Establishing inferior courts.
(18) Concerning the resignation of the president.
(19) Concerning treaties and patronage.
(20) Admitting new religious orders.
(21) Regarding war and peace.
(22) Granting letters of marque and reprisal.
(23) Disposing of land and naval forces.
(24) In time of insurrection ; in regard to the militia.
(25) Permitting entrance of foreign troops.
(26) In case of domestic disturbance.
(27) In the federal district.
(28) Enforcing the constitution.

CHAPTER V. — CONCERNING THE ENACTMENT AND PROMULGATION OF LAWS.

68. Right to initiate legislation.
69. Approved bills.
70. Failure of president to return bill equivalent to approval.
71. Rejected or amended bills.
72. Rejected or amended bills.
73. Form of promulgation.

Section II.—The Executive Power.

CHAPTER I. — OF ITS NATURE AND DURATION.

74. Vesting of executive power.
75. Temporary and permanent default of president.
76. Qualifications of president.
77. Term of office.
78. Cessation of power with cessation of term.
79. Compensation of president and vice-president.
80. Oath of office.

CHAPTER II. — TIME AND MANNER OF THE ELECTION OF PRESIDENT AND VICE-PRESIDENT OF THE NATION.

81. Constitution of electoral college; method of preparing lists.
82. Examination of lists by congress.

83. Case of divided vote.
84. Case of divided vote.
85. Time and publication of election.

CHAPTER III. — POWER OF THE EXECUTIVE.

86. Exclusive and concurrent powers.

CHAPTER IV. — OF THE MINISTERS OF THE EXECUTIVE POWER.

87. Number and office.
88. Responsibility.
89. Limitation of power in department.
90. Reports from departments.
91. Incompatibility of ministerial office with that of senator or deputy.
92. Powers in legislation.
93. Compensation.

Section III.—Of the Judicial Power.

CHAPTER I. — OF ITS NATURE AND DURATION.

94. Vesting of judicial power.
95. No judicial power in president.
96. Term of office and compensation of judges.
97. Qualifications of supreme judges.
98. Oath of office.
99. Regulation of supreme court.

CHAPTER II. — POWER OF THE JUDICIARY.

100. Appellate jurisdiction.
101. Original jurisdiction.
102. Trial by jury.
103. Treason and its punishment.

TITLE II.—THE GOVERNMENT OF THE PROVINCES.

104. General powers of the provinces.
105. Local government.
106. Constitutions of provinces.
107. Treaty-making powers.
108. Concurrent powers of congress and provinces.
109. Prohibitions to provinces.
110. Relation of provincial governors to constitution.

III.

CONSTITUTION OF THE ARGENTINE NATION.

PREAMBLE.

We, the representatives of the people of the Argentine Nation, met in a general Constituent Congress, by the will and election of the component provinces, in compliance with previous compacts, with the object of forming a national union, of guaranteeing justice, insuring domestic tranquility, providing for the common defence, promoting the general welfare, and securing the blessings of liberty to ourselves, to posterity, and to all men who wish to dwell on Argentine soil, invoking the protection of God, fountain of all reason and justice, do ordain, decree and establish the Constitution of this Argentine Nation.

PART FIRST.

CHAPTER I.—DECLARATION, RIGHTS, AND GUARANTEES.

ART. 1. The Argentine Nation adopts for its government the federal republican and representative form as established by the present constitution.

ART. 2. The federal government upholds the Roman Catholic Apostolic religion.

ART. 3. The authorities exercising the functions of government shall reside in that city which is declared by a special law of congress the capital of the Republic, previous cession having been made by the provincial legislatures of territory to be used as a federal district.

ART. 4. The federal government provides for the expenses of the nation from the funds of the national treasury consisting of money accruing from import and export duties [until 1866, in conformity with the enactment of Art. 67, clause I.];[1] the sale or lease of national lands ; postal revenue from mails ; taxes which the General Congress may equitably and proportionately levy on the people; loans and bills of credit by the same congress for the needs of the nation or for enterprises of national benefit.

ART. 5. Each province shall adopt for itself a constitution under the republican representative system, and in accordance with the principles, declarations and guarantees of the national constitution, and which shall insure the administration of justice, municipal government and primary education. Under these conditions the federal government guarantees to each province the enjoyment and exercise of its own institutions.

ART. 6. The federal government invades the territory of the provinces in order to preserve the republican form of government, or to repel invasions, and also at the call of the constitutional authorities, to sustain or to reëstablish them if they have been overturned by sedition, or by invasion from some other province.

ART. 7. Public acts and judicial proceedings of one province are respected in the others; and congress may, by general laws, determine the probationary form of these acts and proceedings, and the legal results which they will produce.

ART. 8. The citizens of each province enjoy all the rights, privileges and immunities rightfully belonging to the citizens of other provinces. Extradition of criminals is a reciprocal obligation imposed upon all the provinces.

ART. 9. In the whole territory of the nation there shall be national custom houses only, in which duties shall be fixed as Congress authorizes.

ART. 10. Within the Republic all articles of domestic production or manufacture, as well as goods and merchandise of all kinds that have been cleared at the custom houses [*aduanas exteriores*] are exempt from taxation.

ART. 11. Articles of domestic and foreign production or manufacture, cattle of all kinds which pass from one province to

[1] See Amendments, p. 46.

another, as well as the carts, boats or beasts used for their transportation, shall be exempt from duties of passage, and no duty can be levied on them beforehand whatever their nature, by the mere act of passing through the territory.

ART. 12. Boats going from one province to another shall not be obliged to enter, anchor[a] and pay duties because of passage; for in no case may one port take precedence of another by means of laws or rules of commerce.

ART. 13. New provinces may be admitted to the nation, but no province shall be erected out of the territory or territories of others, nor shall several provinces unite to form one, without the consent of the provincial legislatures concerned, and also of congress.

ART. 14. All inhabitants of the nation enjoy the following rights in accordance with the laws which regulate their exercise, to wit: to engage in and carry on any legitimate industry; the rights of navigation, commerce, and of petition to the authorities; to enter, to remain in, to pass through, and to leave Argentine territory; to publish opinions through the press without previous censorship; to make use of, and to dispose of property; to form business associations; to exercise any profession in freedom; to teach and to learn.

ART. 15. There are no slaves in the Argentine nation; the few that are here now shall be free upon the adoption of this constitution, and a special law shall regulate the indemnifications which this provision shall necessitate. Any bill of purchase or sale of slaves is considered as criminal, for which the parties concerned, including the clerk or functionary authorizing it, shall be held responsible, and the slaves, whatever be the manner of their introduction, shall be free by the mere act of setting foot on territory of the republic.

ART. 16. The Argentine nation does not recognize prerogatives of blood or of birth; personal privileges and titles of nobility do not exist. All the inhabitants are equal before the

---

[a] All ships entering a port for the purpose of casting anchor there, even though they may have been forced to it by stress of weather, and though they may not while there engage in any trade, must, nevertheless, pay a certain duty which is termed *anclage*.

law, and are eligible to all public employments without other consideration than those of fitness. Equality is the basis of taxation and of admission to public offices.

ART. 17. Property is inviolable, and no inhabitant of the nation can be deprived of it without due process of law. Condemnation of lands for public uses shall be regulated by law, and previously indemnified. Congress alone imposes the taxes which are provided for in Article 4. No personal service can be exacted except by law or by sentence founded on law. All authors or inventors are exclusive proprietors of their work, invention, or discovery, for the length of time accorded by law. Confiscation of goods is blotted out forever from the Argentine penal code. No armed body shall make requisitions or exact aid of any kind.

ART. 18. No inhabitant of the nation can be punished without previous judgment founded on law enacted prior to the institution of the process, nor by special commission,[3] nor shall be brought before judges appointed by a law before the institution of the suit.

No one is compelled to give evidence against himself; nor shall he be arrested except by a written order from the proper authority. Defence of person and property before the law is inviolable. The domicile is inviolable, as are also all correspondence and private papers; and a law shall determine in what cases and with what justification their alienation and confiscation may be undertaken. Penalty of death for political crimes, every kind of torture, and flogging are forever prohibited. The prisons of the nations shall be healthful and clean, with the purpose of keeping safely, not of punishing, the criminals detained in them; and all measures which, under the pretext of precaution, cause undue mortification, shall be laid to the charge of the judge who authorizes them.

ART. 19. Private actions that in no way offend good order

[3] If the parties to a law suit lived in a town at some distance from the residence of the judge, it was customary in Spain for the judge to commission certain persons who would then have authority to try the case. Great abuse was made of this privilege, and in the Spanish liberal constitution of 1812, we find the following provision: "No Spaniard can be judged in civil or criminal suits by any commission, but by a competent tribunal invested with authority by law."

or public morals, nor involve a third party, are reserved to the judgment of God, and are beyond the authority of magistrates. No inhabitant of the nation shall be obliged to do that which the law does not exact, nor deprived of that which the law does not prohibit.

ART. 20. Foreigners in the territory of the nation enjoy all the civil rights of citizens; they may engage in any industry, commerce or profession, possess real estate, buy and sell the same, navigate rivers and coasts, exercise freely their religious belief, make wills and marry according to law. They are not obliged to become citizens or to pay necessary extraordinary contributions. They may obtain the privileges of citizenship by residing two successive years in the nation; but the proper authorities may shorten the time upon application, the applicant pleading special services rendered to the Republic.

ART. 21. Every Argentine citizen is obliged to take up arms in defence of his country and of this constitution, in accordance with the laws passed by congress, and the decrees of the national executive. Naturalized citizens are free to offer or withhold this service for the space of ten years after obtaining their naturalization papers.

ART. 22. The people do not deliberate or govern except through representatives and authorities created by the constitution. Every armed force, or gathering of persons which assumes the rights of the people and petitions in their name, is guilty of the crime of sedition.

ART. 23. In case of internal disturbance or foreign invasion which impedes the exercise of this constitution, and the action of the authorities created by it, the province or territory where the disturbance occurs shall be declared in a state of siege, all constitutional guarantees remaining suspended there. But during the suspension the President of the Republic shall have no power of himself to condemn or to inflict punishment. In such a case his power over persons shall be limited to arrest and transportation from one point to another of the nation, in case they should refuse to leave the country.

ART. 24. Congress shall promote reforms in the present

legislation in all its branches, and shall establish trial by jury.

ART. 25. The federal government shall encourage European immigration, and shall not restrict, limit or oppress with any taxes whatever the entrance into Argentine territory of foreigners who come with the intention of engaging in agriculture, improving industries, and introducing and teaching sciences and arts.

ART. 26. The navigation of all interior rivers of the nation is free to all crafts, subject only to the orders issued by national authority.

ART. 27. The federal government is obliged to confirm its relations of peace and commerce with foreign powers by means of treaties which shall conform to the principles of public right established in this constitution.

ART. 28. The principles, guarantees, and rights recognized in the preceding articles cannot be altered by the laws regulating their action.

ART. 29. Congress cannot grant to the national executive, neither can the provincial legislatures grant to the governors of the provinces, extraordinary powers, or the substance of public power, or concede to them such submission or supremacy that the life, honor and fortunes of any Argentine should be at the mercy of the governors or of any single person. Acts of this nature carry with them an irremediable want of force, and subject those that formulate them to the responsibility and penalties of the most infamous betrayers of their country.

ART. 30. The constitution may be amended in any and all of its parts. The necessity for amendment must be declared by congress by a vote of at least two-thirds of its members; but the amendment shall not be made except by a convention called for the purpose.

ART. 31. This constitution, the laws of the nation which are promulgated by congress in accordance with it, and the treaties with foreign nations shall be the supreme law of the land; the authorities of each province must conform to it, notwithstanding any provision in the provincial laws or constitutions which may be contrary to it, excepting treaties in the province of Buenos Ayres ratified after the peace of November 11, 1859.

ART. 32. The Federal Congress shall not dictate any laws restricting the liberty of the press, or establish over it any federal jurisdiction.

ART. 33. The declarations, rights, and guarantees enumerated by the constitution shall not be regarded as a negative on other rights and guarantees not enumerated, but which arise from the principle of sovereignty of the people and of the republican form of government.

ART. 34. The judges of the federal courts shall not at the same time be judges in the provincial courts; neither can federal service, either in military or civil affairs, give the right of residence in the province where it is performed, and which may not be the customary home of the officer; this applies to the cases of those who accept government employ in the province where they chance to be.

ART. 35. The names adopted successively since 1810 to the present time, to-wit: United Provinces of the River Plate, Argentine Republic, Argentine Confederation, shall henceforward be indiscriminately used to designate the government and territory of the provinces, using the words, Argentine Nation, in the formulation and promulgation of laws.

PART SECOND.—POWERS OF THE NATION.

TITLE I.—FEDERAL GOVERNMENT.

Section I.—The Legislative Power.

ART. 36. The legislative power of the nation shall be vested in a congress composed of two chambers, one of deputies from the nation, the other of senators from the provinces and the capital.

CHAPTER I.—OF THE CHAMBER OF DEPUTIES.

ART. 37. The chamber of deputies shall be composed of representatives elected directly by the people of the provinces and of the capital, which shall be considered for this purpose as electoral districts of a single state; they shall be elected by a simple plurality of votes in the proportion of one for each twenty thousand inhabitants, or any fraction above, less than ten thousand.

ART. 38. The number of deputies for the first legislature shall be in the following proportion: for the province of Buenos Ayres, twelve; for Cordova, six; for Catamarca, three; for Corrientes, four; for Entre Rios, two; for Juijuy, two; for Mendoza, three; for Rioja, two; for Salta, three; for Santiago, four; for San Juan, two; for Santa Fé, two; for San Luis, two; for Tucumán, three.

ART. 39. For the second legislature a general census must be taken and the number of deputies apportioned according to it; this census shall only be taken every ten years.

ART. 40. To be a deputy one must have attained the age of twenty-five years, exercised the rights of citizenship four years, and must be a native of the province which elects him, or have resided there the two years immediately preceding.

ART. 41. For the present legislature, the provincial legislatures shall appoint the manner of direct election of the deputies of the nation; congress shall formulate a general law for succeeding elections.

ART. 42. Deputies shall continue in office four years, and are re-eligible; but half the house shall be renewed every two years, to accomplish which those elected by the first legislature shall by lot select those whose terms shall expire at the end of two years.[4]

---

[4] In Mexico the whole house of deputies is renewed every two years. The election is indirect and by secret ballot. The proportion of deputies is one for each forty thousand inhabitants, or for a fraction that exceeds twenty thousand. Constitution of Mexico, Arts. 52, 53, 55.

In Colombia the members of the lower house are elected for a term of four years, and in the proportion of one for every fifty thousand inhabitants. Constitution of Colombia, Arts. 99, 101.

In Chile the whole house of deputies is renewed every three years. The election is direct, and in the proportion of one for each thirty thousand inhabitants. A property qualification is required for deputies. Constitution of Chile, Art. 17.

In Ecuador deputies are elected for a term of two years, in the proportion of one to each thirty thousand inhabitants, by direct election and secret ballot. Constitution of Ecuador, Arts. 38, 48, 59.

Art. 43. In case of vacancy the governor of the province or of the capital shall order the legal election of a new member.

Art. 44. All laws concerning taxes and the levying of troops shall originate exclusively in the chamber of deputies.

Art. 45. The chamber of deputies has the sole right to impeach before the senate, the president, vice-president, ministers and the members of the supreme and of the inferior courts of the nation, in those cases in which they are responsible for maladministration, or for malfeasance in office, or for common crimes. Before impeachment just cause for the action must be declared by a vote of two-thirds of the members present.

CHAPTER II.—OF THE SENATE.

Art. 46. The Senate shall be composed of two senators from each province, elected by a plurality vote of their respective legislatures; and of two from the capital elected according to the form prescribed for the election of the president of the nation. Each senator shall have one vote.

Art. 47. In order to be be elected senator it is necessary to have attained the age of thirty years, to have been six years a citizen of the nation, to have an annual rent of two thousand [hard] dollars or its equivalent, and to be a native of the province which elects him, or to have resided there two years immediately preceding election.

Art. 48. Senators shall continue in office for nine years and are re-eligible indefinitely; but one-third of the senate shall be renewed every third year, it being decided by lot at the first meeting which ones shall return at the end of the first and second periods of three years.[5]

[5] In Mexico the election of senators is indirect and their term of office is two years. One-half the senate is renewed every two years. Constitution of Mexico, Art. 58.

In Colombia there are three senators from each department elected by the departmental assemblies for a term of six years. The senate is renewed by thirds. Constitution of Colombia, Arts. 93, 95, 175.

In Ecuador the senators are chosen by direct election and secret ballot. There are two senators from each province elected for a term of four years. One half the senate is renewed every two years. Constitution of Chile, Arts. 38, 43, 58.

In Chile the senate is composed of members chosen directly by the people of the provinces in the proportion of one senator to every three deputies for a term of six years. Constitution of Chile, Arts. 22, 23.

ART. 49. The vice-president of the nation shall be the president of the senate; but he shall not have a vote except in the case of a tie.

ART. 50. The senate shall appoint a president *pro tempore* who will preside in the absence of the vice-president, or when the latter is acting as the president of the nation.

ART. 51. The senate shall act as a public court for the trial of those impeached by the chamber of deputies, its members taking oath beforehand. If the president of the nation is impeached the president of the supreme court shall preside over the senate. No one shall be convicted without the vote of two-thirds of the members present.

ART. 52. Judgment shall not extend further than to removal and disqualification to hold any office of honor, trust or profit in the nation. But the party convicted shall nevertheless be subject to indictment, judgment and punishment according to law before the ordinary tribunals.

ART. 53. It is also the duty of the senate to authorize the president of the nation to declare any or several places in the republic in a state of siege, in case of foreign invasion.

ART. 54. In case of vacancies caused by death or resignation, or any other cause, the government of the province from which the senator was elected shall proceed immediately to the election of a new member.

CHAPTER III.—PROVISIONS RELATING TO BOTH HOUSES.

ART. 55. Both houses shall meet in ordinary session every year, from the first of May until the thirtieth of September. They may also be convoked in extraordinary session, or prorogued by the president.

ART. 56. Each house is the judge of the elections, rights, titles and qualifications of its members. Neither house shall do business without an absolute majority of its members; but a smaller number may compel the attendance of the absent members in such a manner and under such penalties as each house may provide.

ART. 57. Both houses shall open and close their sessions

simultaneously. Neither house during a session shall, without the consent of the other, adjourn for more than three days.

ART. 58. Each house shall make its own rules, and, with the concurrence of two-thirds, may punish any member for disorderly behavior in the exercise of his functions, or expel him because of moral or physical disabilities incurred after taking his seat, and sufficient to exclude him from membership; but a majority of those present will be sufficient to pass on cases of negligence in the discharge of duty.

ART. 59. The senators and deputies upon taking their seats, must take an oath to discharge with fidelity their duty, and to do everything in conformity with the provisions of this constitution.

ART. 60. No member of congress shall be indicted, questioned by law, or held responsible for the opinions or speeches which he delivers during his term of office as legislator.

ART. 61. No senator or deputy from the day of his election until his term ceases can be subject to arrest except in the case of detection in the act of committing a crime deserving punishment by death, by penalty involving disgrace, or by other personal punishment;[6] concerning which an account shall be given before his house, with a summary of the act.

ART. 62. When a formal complaint in writing is made before the ordinary justices, against any senator or deputy, and when the case has been investigated in open court, each house may by a two-third vote suspend the accused from the exercise of his functions, and hand him over to the judge under whose jurisdiction the case falls.

[6] "*Pena de muerte, infamante ú otra aflictiva.*" At the time of the adoption of this constitution there were two modes of capital punishment established by law in Spain, the *garrote* for civilians, and shooting for military criminals. There were three modes of garroting; ordinary garroting, when the criminal went to the place of execution mounted on a mule, with his coat fastened about him; infamous garroting, when the criminal must ride to his death on a jack-ass, with his coat unfastened; garrote for the nobility, when the criminal had the privilege of mounting a saddled horse, and could wear a black cloak, and in special cases was permitted to have the place of execution draped in mourning. Hanging, as a death penalty, was abolished in 1832.

Pena infamante is that form of punishment which dishonors the person subjected to it, as hanging, public shame and scourging.

Pena aflictiva or punishment of the person (as distinguished from a fine), is such as scourging, banishment, imprisonment for more than six months, etc.

ART. 63. Each house may require the presence of the ministers of the executive power, to receive from them any explanations or information that may be deemed necessary.

ART. 64. No member of congress can receive office or commission from the executive power without the previous consent of his house, except in the case of officers of the port.

ART. 65. Regular clergy cannot be members of congress, neither can provincial governors be elected to congress during their term of office.

ART. 66. Senators and deputies are remunerated for their services from the national treasury by an amount which shall be determined by law.

CHAPTER IV.—POWERS OF CONGRESS.

ART. 67. It belongs to congress
(1) To legislate concerning custom houses [*aduanas exteriores*] and to establish import duties, which duties, as well as the valuation upon which they are based, shall be uniform throughout the nation; it being understood that this, as well as other national duties, may be paid in the currency of the respective provinces, to the full value. To establish equally the duties on exports [until 1866 at which time they will cease as a national tax, the same being prohibited as provincial taxes].[7]
(2) To impose direct taxes for a definite time and in equal proportion throughout the whole territory of the nation, as long as the defence, common security and general good of the state demand it.
(3) To contract loans on the credit of the nation.
(4) To direct the use and the sale of national lands.
(5) To establish and regulate a national bank in the capital, and its branches in the provinces with power to issue bills of credit.
(6) To arrange for the foreign and domestic debt of the nation.

See Amendments, page 46.

(7) To fix annually an estimate of the national administrative expenses, and to approve or disapprove the budget of expenditures.

(8) To grant sums from the national treasury to those provinces whose revenues do not cover, according to their estimate, the ordinary expenses.

(9) To regulate the free navigation of interior rivers, to establish such ports as are necessary; to create and abolish custom houses, with the exception of those custom houses which exist in each province at the time of their incorporation.

(10) To coin money, to fix its value and that of foreign money, to adopt a uniform system of weights and measures throughout the country.

(11) To dictate the civil, commercial, penal and mining codes, without allowing such codes to alter local judicature, making their application correspond to the federal or the provincial tribunals according as the matters or persons fall under their respective jurisdictions; and especially general laws for the whole nation, concerning naturalization and citizenship, in accordance with the principle of natural citizenship; also laws concerning bankruptcy, counterfeiting of securities and current coin of the state; and those laws requiring the establishment of trial by jury.

(12) To regulate commerce by land and by sea, with foreign nations and between the provinces.

(13) To regulate and establish the general post-offices and post-roads of the nation.

(14) To fix definitely the territorial limits of the nation and those of the provinces, to erect new provinces and to determine by special legislation the organization, administration and government to be established in the national territory which is outside the limits assigned to the provinces.

(15) To provide for the security of the frontiers, to preserve the treaty of peace with the Indians and to promote their conversion to Catholicism.

(16) To provide for all that conduces to the prosperity of the country, to the advancement and well-being of all the provinces, and to the progress of education, prescribing plans for general and university instruction, promoting industry, immigration, the building of railroads and navigable canals, the colonization of national lands, the introduction and establishment of new industries, the importation of foreign capital, and the exploration of interior rivers by laws protecting their banks, by temporary concessions of privilege, and by the offer of rewards.

(17) To establish courts inferior to the supreme court of justice, to create and abolish offices, to prescribe their powers, to give pensions, to confer honors, and to concede general amnesty.

(18) To act upon the resignation of president or vice-president of the Republic, to declare a new election, and to examine and verify it.

(19) To approve or to disapprove of the treaties concluded with other nations and the covenants made with the Apostolic Chair, and to regulate the exercise of patronage throughout the whole nation.

(20) To admit within the territory of the nation other religious orders besides those already existing.

(21) To authorize the executive power to declare war or to make peace.

(22) To grant letters of marque and reprisal.

(23) To dispose of the land and naval forces in times of peace and war; to make rules and regulations for the government of said forces.

(24) To authorize the summoning of the militia of all the provinces, or parts of them, when the execution of the laws of the nation so require, or to suppress insurrections and repel invasions. To provide for the organizing, arming, and disciplining of said militia and the administration and government of that part of it which may be employed in the service of the nation, leaving to the

provinces respectively the appointment of officers and the responsibility of establishing the military discipline prescribed by congress.

(25) To permit the entrance of foreign troops into the territory of the nation and the departure of national forces.

(26) To declare in a state of siege any or several points in the nation in case of domestic disturbance; to continue or suspend the state of siege declared by the executive during a recess of congress.

(27) To exercise exclusive legislation over all the territory of the national capital and those places acquired by purchase or cession in any of the provinces, for the purpose of establishing fortresses, arsenals, magazines or other establishments of national service.

(28) To make all laws and regulations which shall be necessary for carrying into execution the foregoing powers, and all other powers vested by this constitution in the government of the Argentine Nation.

CHAPTER V.— CONCERNING THE ENACTMENT AND PROMULGATION OF LAWS.

ART. 68. All laws may originate in either house on the initiative of its respective members, or of the executive power, except those laws relating to subjects treated in Art. 44.

ART. 69. If a bill is approved by the originating house it shall pass for discussion to the other house. If it pass both houses it shall go to the executive, and if it obtains his approval it shall be promulgated as law.

ART. 70. Every bill not returned by the executive within ten working days shall be considered a law.

ART. 71. No bill failing to pass either house can be reconsidered in any session of the same year. But if it is amended by the revising house it shall be returned to the originating house; if in this house an absolute majority approve the amendments it shall be sent to the executive power of the nation. If the amendments be disapproved the bill shall be returned again to the revising house, and if there the amendments be approved a second time by a majority of two-thirds of the members, the bill shall pass again to the originating house, but this house will not be understood to approve the amendments without the concurrence of two-thirds of the members present.

ART. 72. If a bill be rejected in whole or in part by the executive power, it returns with his objections to the house in which it originated; this house shall discuss it anew, and if it is passed by a two-thirds vote it shall go a second time to the other house. If it pass both houses by a two-thirds vote the bill becomes a law and goes to the executive power for promulgation. The votes in both houses in this case shall be by yeas and nays; the names of the persons voting for and against the bill, together with the objections of the executive power, shall be published immediately by the press. If the house disagree over the objections the bill cannot be reconsidered in any session of the same year.

ART. 73. In the promulgation of laws the following formula shall be used: The senate and the chamber of deputies of the Argentine nation, in congress assembled, etc., decree or sanction as law.[8]

[8] In Mexico the right of initiative belongs to the president, to the deputies and senators, and to the legislatures of the states. Laws may originate in either house, except those bills which treat of loans, taxes, or imports, or of the recruiting of troops, all of which must be discussed first in the house of deputies.

Bills presented by the president, by the legislatures of the states, or by deputations from the same, shall pass immediately to a committee.

Bills presented by deputies or senators are subjected to the same procedure as in the Argentine constitution, with the following exceptions: (1) If a bill is rejected only in part, or modified, or receives additions by the house of revision, the new discussion in the house where it originated shall treat only of the rejected part, or of the amendments or additions, without being able to alter in any manner the articles approved. (2) If in the second revision the house of revision should insist by an absolute majority on the amendments in each, the whole bill shall not be again presented until the following session, unless both houses agree by an absolute majority that the law shall be issued only with the articles approved. (3) When a bill has been rejected wholly or in part by the executive and returned to the house where it originated, it will require confirmation only by an absolute majority, instead of by a two-thirds vote. Constitution of Mexico, Arts. 65, 66 and 71.

In Colombia the right of initiative belongs to deputies, senators and the ministers of the government. The house of deputies has exclusive right to originate all laws for the levying of taxes and for the organization of the public ministry.

All legislative acts must have passed three readings and been adopted in

Section II.—The Executive Power.

CHAPTER I.—OF ITS NATURE AND DURATION.

ART. 74. The executive power of the nation shall be exercised by a citizen with the title of "President of the Argentine Nation."

ART. 75. In case of the illness, absence from the capital, death, resignation or dereliction of the president, the executive power shall be exercised by the vice-president of the nation. In case of dereliction, death, resignation or inability of the president and vice-president of the nation, congress shall determine what public functionary shall fill the office of president, until the cause of inability has been removed, or a new president is elected.

ART. 76. To be elected president or vice-president of the nation it is necessary to have been born in Argentine territory, or to be the son of a native citizen if born in a foreign country, to be of the Roman Catholic Apostolic communion, and to possess the other qualifications required for senators.

ART. 77. The president and vice-president continue in office six years; and they cannot be re-elected without the interval of one term.[9]

each house, on three different days, by a majority of the members before they pass to the government for approval. No act shall be voted on its third reading without the presence of an absolute majority of the members. The president is allowed six days in which to return a bill with objections when it contains no more than fifty articles; he is given ten days to consider a bill containing from fifty-one to two hundred articles, and fifteen days for a bill of more than two hundred articles. Constitution of Colombia, Arts. 80, 81, 82, 86, 102.

In Chile laws concerning amnesty must originate in the senate. The right of initiative belongs to senators, deputies, and to the president by means of a message. The procedure in the enactment of laws is the same as in Argentina, except that the president is allowed fifteen days for the consideration of a bill. Constitution of Chile, Arts. 31, 35.

In Ecuador besides senators, deputies and the president, the Supreme Court has also the right of initiative in matters pertaining to the administration of justice. If a bill passes both houses it is sent to the executive, who must return it within nine days, or in case of urgency within three days. If his objections concern the bill as a whole it shall be laid aside and not brought up again until the following legislature. In every case an absolute majority is required. Constitution of Ecuador, Arts. 64-71.

[9] This provision was also adopted in the constitution of the Confederate States of America, 1862.

Art. 78. The president of the nation ceases to have power the very day that his term of six years expires; and no event whatever which may have interrupted this term can be a reason for prolonging it.

Art. 79. The president and vice-president shall receive from the national treasury a salary, which cannot be increased or diminished during their term of office. During this period they cannot hold any other office or receive any emolument from the nation or from any province.

Art. 80. Upon taking possession of their office, the president and vice-president, shall, in the presence of the president of the senate take the following oath [the first time the oath must be taken in the presence of the presiding officer of the Constituent Congress], congress being assembled; "I, N. N., swear in the name of God and the Holy Evangelists to execute with loyalty and patriotism the office of president [or vice-president] of the nation, and faithfully to preserve and cause to be preserved the Constitution of the Argentine Nation. If I do not thus may God and the Nation call me to account."[10]

[10] In Mexico the qualifications for president are, that he must be a Mexican by birth, that he must be thirty-five years old, that he must not belong to the ecclesiastical order, and that he must reside in the country at the time of his election. His term of office is four years; he may be re-elected, but is ineligible for a third term until an interval of four years has elapsed. There is no vice-president. In case of vacancy, the president or vice-president of the senate or of the permanent commission assumes the presidential office until a new election is held. The new election must be held within three months of the occurrence of the vacancy. Constitution of Mexico, Arts. 77, 78, 79.

In Colombia the qualifications for president are, that he must be a native Colombian, that he must be more than thirty years of age, and that he must have an income of at least two thousand two hundred dollars. The term of office is six years. Constitution of Colombia, Arts. 114, 115.

In Ecuador the term of office of president and vice-president is four years. They are not eligible for election to a second term until a period of eight years has elapsed. During this time the president cannot be elected to the office of vice-president, or *vice versa*. No relative of the president in the first or second degree can be elected to succeed him. Constitution of Ecuador, Arts. 81, 86 and 87.

In Chile the presidential term is five years; no second term is permitted unless a period of five years has elapsed. There is no vice-president, and in case of vacancy the Minister of the Interior assumes the presidential office. Writs for a new election must be issued within ten days after the vacancy occurs. Constitution of Chile, Arts. 50, 52 and 55.

CHAPTER II.—OF THE TIME AND MANNER OF THE ELECTION OF THE PRESIDENT AND VICE-PRESIDENT OF THE NATION.

ART. 81. The manner of electing the president and vice-president of the nation shall be as follows : the capital and each one of the provinces shall appoint by direct election an assembly of electors equal to twice the total number of the deputies and senators which they elect to Congress, with the same qualifications, and according to the forms prescribed for the election of deputies. No deputy nor senator, nor any one holding an office of profit under the federal government can be an elector. The electors shall assemble in the capital of the nation and in the capitals of their respective provinces, four months before the close of the existing administration and shall proceed to elect the president and vice-president by means of sealed ballots. They shall name in their ballots the person voted for as president, and in distinct ballots the person voted for as vice-president. They shall make two lists of all persons voted for as president, and two other lists of all persons voted for as vice-president, with the number of votes for each. These lists shall be signed by the electors and two of these lists [one of each kind] shall be transmitted, closed and sealed, to the president of the provincial legislature, and in the case of the capital to the president of the municipality, in whose offices they shall be deposited and locked ; and the other two shall be transmitted to the President of the Senate [the first time to the President of the Constituent Congress].

ART. 82. The President of the Senate [the first time the President of the Constituent Congress] shall open the lists in the presence of both Houses. The secretaries, together with four members of congress chosen by lot, shall proceed immediately to examine and to announce the number of votes which result in favor of each candidate for the Presidency and Vice-Presidency of the nation. Those who have in both cases the absolute majority of votes shall be immediately proclaimed President and Vice-President.

ART. 83. In the case of a divided vote when there is no absolute majority, congress shall elect among the two having the greatest number of votes. If the first plurality includes more than two persons, congress shall elect from among all these. If the first majority includes only one person, and the second includes two or more, congress shall elect from among all those having the first and second majorities.

ART. 84. This election shall be affected by the absolute plurality and by a viva voce vote. If, after the first ballot, there should result no absolute majority, another ballot shall be taken uniting the votes on those persons who, in the first ballot, had obtained the greatest number of votes. In case of a tie, the ballot shall be taken again, and if another tie should result, the President of the Senate [the first time the President of the Constituent Congress] shall decide. The inspection and verification of these elections cannot take place unless three-fourths of all the members of congress are present.

ART. 85. The election of President and Vice-President of the nation should take place during a single session of congress, and the result, together with the electoral acts, should be immediately published by the public press.

CHAPTER III.—POWERS OF THE EXECUTIVE.

ART. 86. The President of the nation has the following powers:

(1) He is supreme head of the nation, and has in his care the general administration of the country.

(2) He has power to enact such laws and regulations as are necessary for the carrying out of the laws of the nation, taking care not to alter their spirit by means of regulating exceptions.

(3) He is the direct and local head of the capital of the nation.

(4) He takes part in the formation of laws in accordance with the constitution, and approves and promulgates them.

(5) He appoints, with the consent of the senate, the magistrates of the supreme court, and of the inferior courts.

(6) He may grant reprieves or pardon for offences subject to the jurisdiction of the federal courts, prior to information brought by the corresponding court, except in cases of impeachment by the chamber of deputies.

(7) He grants pensions, accepts resignations, grants leaves of absence, and *goces de monte-pios* [11] in conformity with the law of the nation.

(8) He exercises the rights of national patronage in the conferring of bishoprics to the cathedral churches, upon the proposal of one-third of the senate.

(9) With the concurrence of the supreme court he concedes pass or withhold the decrees of the councils, the bulls, briefs, and rescripts of the Supreme Pontiff of Rome ; requiring for them a law when they contain general and permanent provisions.

(10) With the consent of the senate he appoints and removes ministers plenipotentiary and charges d'affairs ; and by himself appoints and removes accredited ministers, and their attachés, consular agents and others employed in the administration whose appointment is not otherwise provided in this constitution.

(11) He opens the annual sessions of congress, both houses being assembled for that purpose in the hall of the senate; and on this occasion he must give a report of the state of the nation, of the reforms assured by the constitution and recommends to their consid-

---

[11] *Goces de monte-pios*, privilege of *monte-pios*. The *monte-pio* of Spain is identical with the French *mont-de-piété*. In the middle ages these institutions were established by the monks to prevent the poor people from having recourse to the Jews and other usurers. Their object was to render aid in cases of extreme necessity, for which service full recompense was made later. The first *mont-de-piété* was established in Rome in the latter half of the fifteenth century, and soon developed into a flourishing bank. Later one was established Paris, and then others sprang up. It became the custom to require exorbitant securities, and the *mont-de-piété* lost its first character of a benevolent institution and became a money-making establishment. Laws were made regulating the amount of money that could be borrowed from the *mont-de-piété* and also the amount of the security which could be demanded by the *mont-de-piété*. There is no institution in England or the United States corresponding to this, but the monte-pio of Spain and of Latin-America is identical with it. There are also such pawnshops, if we may so call them, in Belgium and Holland.

eration those measures which he judges necessary and expedient.

(12) He prorogues the ordinary sessions of congress, or calls extraordinary meetings when grave questions of order or progress demand it.

(13) He orders the collection of the national revenues and directs their investment in accordance with law, or with the estimate of the national expenses.

(14) He concludes and confirms treaties of peace, of commerce, of navigation, of alliance, of limits, and of neutrality; contracts and other negotiations required for the maintenance of amicable relations with foreign powers; he receives their ministers and admits their consuls.

(15) He is commander-in-chief of all land and naval forces of the nation.

(16) With the consent of the senate, he fills, in the order of rank, the higher military and naval offices; and in the field of battle by his own authority.

(17) He disposes of all military forces on land and sea, and regulates their distribution and organization according to the necessities of the nation.

(18) He declares war, and grants letters of marque and reprisal, with the authority and approbation of congress.

(19) With the concurrence of the senate, and in case of foreign attack, he may declare any or various points in the nation to be in a state of siege for a limited time. In case of interior commotion, he only has this power during a recess of congress, because this is an attribute which belongs exclusively to that body. The president exercises it with the limitations provided in *Art. 23*.

(20) He may require any information which he deems necessary from the chiefs of all the departments of administration, and through them from other officials, which information they are obliged to furnish.

(21) He may not leave the territory of the capital without

the permission of congress. During a recess, he may do so without permission, but only for reasons of the gravest public importance.

(22) The President has power to fill those vacancies which require the consent of the senate, and which may occur during a recess of the same, by temporary appointments which shall expire at the close of the next legislature.

CHAPTER IV.— OF THE MINISTERS OF THE EXECUTIVE POWER.

ART. 87. Five ministers secretaries, to wit : of the Interior ; of Foreign Affairs ; of the Treasury ; of Justice ; of Education and Public Instruction ; of War and Navy ; shall have in their charge the dispatch of the affairs of the nation, and shall corroborate and legalize the acts of the President by means of their seal, without which requisite these acts will fail of their effect. A law shall define the authority of the several ministers.

ART. 88. Every minister is responsible for the acts which he authorizes ; and conjointly with his colleagues for those which he approves.[12]

[12] In the Mexican constitution, there is the following provision for a cabinet : " For the dispatch of the business of the administrative department of the Federation, there shall be the number of secretaries which the congress may establish by law, which shall provide for the distribution of business, and prescribe what shall be in charge of each secretary.

" To be a secretary of the cabinet, it is required that one shall be a Mexican citizen by birth, in the exercise of his rights, and fully twenty-five years old." Constitution of Mexico, Arts. 86 and 87.

In Colombia, the president exercises the executive powers with the "indispensable coöperation of the ministers." The number, designation and precedence of these ministers is determined by law. The ministers, together with the president, form the government, and the ministers are the government's organs of communication with congress. In this Republic, there is also a council of state composed of seven members ; the vice-president of the republic and six voting members appointed according to law. These councillors hold their office for four years, one-half being renewed every two years. The duties of the council are to act as the supreme consulting body of the government in matters of administration, although their opinions shall not be binding, except in the case of a vote for the commutation of the death penalty. They have also certain legislative and judicial powers. Constitution of Colombia, Arts. 59, 132, 134, 136, 138, and 141.

In the constitution of Ecuador, there is the following provision : " For the exercise of his power, the president of the republic shall have such secretaries of state as the law may determine." Besides the secretaries of state, there is also a council of state composed of the vice-president of the republic, the secretaries of state, the fiscal

ART. 89. In no case can ministers alone resolve on anything which takes exception to the economic or administrative system of their respective departments.

ART. 90. When congress has convened, the ministers of state should present a detailed report of the state of the nation in that which concerns the business of their respective departments.

ART. 91. Ministers cannot be either senators or deputies unless they resign from office.

ART. 92. Ministers may attend the meetings of congress and take part in debate, but may not vote.

ART. 93. They shall receive for their services a compensation fixed by law, which cannot be increased or diminished to the favor or to the prejudice of those in office.

Section III.—Of the Judicial Power.
CHAPTER I.—OF ITS NATURE AND DURATION.

ART. 94. The judicial power of the nation shall be exercised by one supreme court of justice, and by such inferior courts as congress shall establish in the territory of the nation.

ART. 95. In no case can the president of the nation exercise judicial functions, take cognizance of pending cases, or of those that have been already concluded.

ART. 96. The judges of the supreme court and of the inferior courts of the nation shall remain in office during good behavior, and shall receive for their services a compensation which shall be determined by law, and which cannot be dimin-

---

minister of the supreme court, two senators, one deputy, one ecclesiastic, and three citizens possessing the qualifications required for a senator. At each biennial meeting congress elects the seven last named. This council of state has consultative power; it may also approve or disapprove of the acts of the executive when congress is not in session. Constitution of Ecuador, Arts. 104, 105 and 106.

In Chile, the provision for the ministers is practically the same as in Ecuador. In this republic, there is also a council of state. It is composed of three councillors elected by the senate, and three by the chamber of deputies, and of five councillors appointed by the president. These latter must be, a member of the Supreme Court of Justice, an ecclesiastic, a general in the army or navy, a chief in some office of the treasury, an individual who has at sometime discharged the offices of Minister of State, diplomatic agent, intendant, governor, or city councillor. The powers of the council are more extended in this republic than in the others. Constitution of Chile, Arts. 93, 94 and 95.

ished in any manner whatever while they remain in the exercise of their office.

ART. 97. No one can be a member of the supreme court of justice unless he is a lawyer of eight years standing in the nation, and possesses all the qualifications required for a senator.

ART. 98. At the first installation of the supreme court, the persons appointed shall take oath befor the president of the nation to discharge their duties by administering justice well and lawfully, and in conformity with the provisions of the constitution. Afterwards they shall take the oath before the president of the court.

ART. 99. The supreme court shall regulate its interior and economic affairs and shall appoint all its inferior officers.[13]

CHAPTER II.—POWERS OF THE JUDICIARY.

ART. 100. The jurisdiction of the supreme court and of the inferior courts of the nation extends to the taking cognizance of

[13] The structure of the Mexican judiciary differs somewhat from that of the Argentine. The judicial power is vested in a supreme court of justice, and in district and circuit courts. The number of judges of the supreme court is prescribed, eleven judges, four supernumaries, one fiscal, and one attorney-general. Their term of office is six years, and their election indirect in the first degree. The qualifications are less exacting than in the Argentine; to be a judge one must "be learned in the science of the law in the judgment of the electors, more than thirty-five years old, and a Mexican citizen by birth, in the exercise of his rights." Constitution of Mexico, Arts. 90, 91, 92 and 93.

In Colombia, the constitution provides for a supreme court for superior district tribunals and "such other tribunals and inferior courts as may be established by law." The number of judges is limited to seven, who hold office during good behavior and are appointed by the president. The qualifications are that they must be Colombians by birth, thirty-five years old, and must have presided as judges in one of the superior district tribunals, or have pursued, with credit, the profession of law for five years at least, or have been professors of jurisprudence in some public institution. Constitution of Colombia, Arts. 60, 146, 147 and 150.

In Ecuador, the constitution provides for a supreme court, for superior courts, for trial by jury, and for "such tribunals and courts as the constitution and the law establish." The term of office is six years, with the privilege of re-election indefinitely. The judges of the supreme court are elected by congress. Their qualifications are the same as in the Argentine. Constitution of Ecuador, Arts. 107, 108 and 110.

The constitution of Chile provides that all civil and criminal cases pertain exclusively to tribunals established by law. The term of office of judges in the superior court is during good behavior; they are appointed by the president. A law determines their qualifications. Constitution of Chile, Arts. 73, clause 7, 99, 101 and 103.

and investigating all cases which relate to points touched upon in the constitution, and to all laws of the nation, with the exception made by clause 11 of Art. 67, and to treaties with foreign nations; to cases concerning ambassadors, public ministers and foreign consuls; to all cases of admiralty and maritime jurisdiction; to all cases to which the nation is a party; to all cases arising between two or more provinces, between a province and citizens of another province, between citizens of different provinces, between a province or its citizens and a foreign citizen or state.

ART. 101. In these cases the supreme court shall exercise appellate jurisdiction according to the rules and exceptions prescribed by congress; but in all affairs concerning ambassadors, ministers and foreign consuls, and in any case where a province is a party it shall exercise original jurisdiction exclusively.

ART. 102. All ordinary criminal cases which do not arise from the right of impeachment granted to the chamber of deputies, shall be tried before juries as soon as this institution is established in the republic. The trial of such cases shall be held in the same province where the act is committed; but if it is committed outside the limits of the nation against the law of nations, congress shall determine by a particular law the place where justice shall be administered.

ART. 103. Treason against the nation shall consist only in taking up arms against, or uniting with its enemies and lending them help and succor. Congress shall determine, by a special law, the penalty for this crime; but it shall not work corruption of blood, nor shall the opprobrium of the criminal extend to any relative of any degree.

TITLE II.—THE GOVERNMENT OF THE PROVINCES.

ART. 104. The provinces reserve all powers which are not delegated by this constitution to the federal government, and which have not been expressly reserved by special treaties at the time of its incorporation.

ART. 105. They have their own local institutions and govern themselves by them. They elect their governors, legislators and other functionaries of the province without the intervention of the federal government.

ART. 106. Each province frames its own constitution in accordance with the dispositions in Art. 5.

ART. 107. With the consent of congress, provinces may enter into treaties, with the object of administering justice, for economic interests and works of common profit; they may promote, by means of protective laws, industry, immigration, building of railroads and navigable canals, colonization of lands belonging to the province; the introduction and establishment of new industries, the importation of foreign capital, and the exploration of rivers.

ART. 108. The provinces do not exercise any power which is delegated to the nation. They cannot enter into treaties of a political character; nor make laws relating to commerce, nor to interior or foreign navigation; nor establish provincial custom houses, nor coin money, nor establish banks with the power of issuing bank-notes, without the authority of congress; nor have they the power to dictate civil, commercial, penal or mining codes after such laws have been passed by congress; nor to dictate special laws concerning citizenship and naturalization, bankruptcy, counterfeiting of coin or securities of the state; nor to lay any duty of tonnage; nor to arm ships of war, nor to raise troops except in case of invasion, or such times of imminent peril that admit of no delay, afterwards rendering an account to the federal government; nor to appoint or receive foreign agents; nor to admit any new religious orders.

ART. 109. No province can declare or make war with another province. Its complaints must be submitted to the supreme court of justice and adjusted by it. These acts of hostility are acts of civil war, belonging to the category of sedition or tumult, that the federal government ought to choke and repress according to law.

ART. 110. The governors of the province are the legitimate agents of the federal government, for the purpose of enforcing the observance of the constitution and the laws of the nation.

Done in accordance with the reforms sanctioned by the National Convention, in consequence of the provisions of Art. 9, of the convention of June 6th of the current year.

To be executed and published throughout the territory of the nation.

Assembly hall of the National Convention, in the city of Santa Fé, on the 25th day of the month of September, in the year 1860.

MARIANO FRAGÚEIRO.

LUCIO V. MANSILLO,
Secretary.

CARLOS M. SARAVIA,
Secretary.

DEPARTMENT OF THE INTERIOR. PARANÁ, October 1, 1860.

To be accepted as the fundamental law of the Argentine Nation, to be published and circulated.

DERQUI,
JUAN PUJOL,
EMILIO DE ALVEAR,
NORBEETO DE LA RIESTRA,
JOSÉ S. DE OLMOS,
JOSÉ MARIA FRANCIA.

AMENDMENTS.

The National Convention enacts the following :

1. That part of Article 4 of the national constitution, which reads : "Until 1866 in conformity with the enactments of Art. 67, Clause I." shall be suppressed, and instead said article shall be rendered in the following terms : "The federal government provides for the expenses of the nation from the funds of the national treasury, consisting of money accruing from import and export duties; the sale or lease of national lands; postal revenue from mails; taxes which the general congress may equitably and proportionately levy on the people ; loans and bills of credit by the same congress for the needs of the nation, or for enterprises of national benefit."

2. Likewise the last part of Clause 1, Article 67, which reads : "Until 1866, at which time they will cease as a national tax, the same being prohibited as provisional taxes," shall be suppressed, and therefore said clause will read : "To legislate concerning custom houses (aduanas exteriores) and to establish import duties, which duties, as well as the valuations upon which they are based, shall be uniform throughout the nation ; it being understood that this as well as other national duties, may be paid in the currency of the respective provinces to the full value. To establish equably the duties on exports."

3. To be communicated to the federal government of the republic, that it may be executed in all the territory of the nation, and to be published.

Assembly Hall of the National Convention in the city of Santa Fé, on the twelfth day of month of September of 1866.

<p style="text-align:right">MARIANO FRAGÚEIRO, President.
JUAN A. BARBEITO, <i>Secretary.</i></p>

J. J. MONTES DE OCA, *Secretary.*

BIBLIOGRAPHY.

American State Papers; Foreign Affairs, Vol. IV.
Arosemena: Constituciones Politicas.
Account of Rio de la Plata: London, 1825.
Cervantes; Estudios sobre el Rio de la Plata.
Child; South American Republics.
Conquest of La Plata; Hukluyt Society.
Consular Reports, U. S.
Dictionaire de l'Economie Politique.
Escriche; Diccionario de Legislacion.
Turner; Argentina and the Argentines.
Winsor; Narrative and Critical History of America.
Periodicals:
    London Times.
    Macmillan's Magazine, Sept., 1890.
    North American Review.
    Saturday Review, March and July, 1890.

Part II.

The Constitution of the United States of Brazil

NOTE.

The Constitution of Brazil has been translated from the Portugese and the translation compared with that issued by the Bureau of American Republics.

I.

HISTORICAL INTRODUCTION.

The history of all the Spanish American Republics is much alike. In each we hear the story of discovery, of brilliant and cruel conquest, of oppressive colonial rule, of awakening independence, of long struggling for freedom, and of energetic though often misdirected efforts to establish constitutional government. The history of the Portuguese American republic differs from that of her sisters in many respects, but the same strong family traits are there, and democratic instincts have brought her out of imperialism into republicanism.

A sudden storm at sea gave Brazil to Portugal. This immense country was first discovered by a Spaniard, Vicente Yañez Pinzon, in January of 1500. He landed and solemnly took possession in the name of his king. Just two months afterwards a great expedition was fitted out by Emanuel, King of Portugal, and placed under command of one Cabrál. The purpose of this expedition was to round the southern coast of Africa and sail to the Indian Seas. Before they were many days out a tempest arose, and the fleet was blown far out in the western ocean. After some days, on April 24, 1500, they sighted an unknown country; it was Brazil. Spain was forced to give up her claim, for according to the Bull of Alexander VI., and by the convention of Tordesillas [June 4, 1494], the dividing line between Portuguese and Spanish possessions had been fixed at 47° 32' 56". All discoveries east of this line must belong to Portugal, those west should belong to Spain.

The fact that this territory belonged to Portugal gave a different stamp to its colonization and to its development. Portugal was prosperous, rich, and essentially a commercial country. In contrast to warlike Spain, she was of a peaceful disposition, and was less impregnated with that dark fanaticism that had been engendered by the long struggle with the Saracens. Therefore Brazil was not invaded by a Cortéz burning with loyal ambition to add new kingdoms to Spain, or by a Pizarro spurred on by love of gain to commit unnameable cruelties. The settlement and colonization were carried on in a desultory sort of way, and no special administrative effort was made until 1576, when all the Portuguese colonies in America were united under one captain-general, whose residence was fixed at Bahia. In 1763, the capital was changed to Rio de Janeiro, and the captain-general received the title of viceroy of Portugal. The population of the vice-royalty consisted of Portuguese adventurers and merchants, of large numbers of Jews banished from Portugal by the Inquisition, of negro slaves, and of criminals.

Commercial restrictions, religious intolerance, grievous defects in the administrative system, no public education, and a bitterly conservative spirit towards foreigners, were the characteristics of Portuguese America. Therefore, during the long years of the colonial period it made but slight advance, and improved but little its great opportunities. However, the hour of independence struck simultaneously for it and for its Spanish-American neighbors.

In 1807 the French army, under Marshal Junot, invaded Portugal with the design of seizing the royal family. The prince regent, Dom Juan, had done everything in his power to avert the coming storm, but in vain. Napoleon had determined to add the whole of the Peninsula to his other conquests, and on the 29th of November his army was looking down upon Lisbon. Then the prince regent resolved upon emigration to Brazil. Everything of value was hastily embarked with the royal family, and the fleet, escorted by an English squadron, set sail for America. The royal exiles were received with enthusiasm, and their presence proved a real and important advantage to the vice-royalty. One of Dom Juan's first acts was to open the ports to commerce with all nations. He accomplished many other reforms, made necessary by the fact that a nation so far away from the seat of government ought in many ways to regulate its own affairs. By recognizing this principle he naturally fostered the idea of independence, which had already taken root in the minds of the people. The most important reform was the decree of December, 1815, by which Brazil was declared to be no longer a colony, but an integral part of the "United Kingdom of Portugal, Algarves, and Brazil." Shortly after this the queen mother died and the prince regent succeeded to the throne as Dom Juan VI. The revolutionary movement in Portugal in 1821 made it necessary for the king to leave Brazil. He appointed his son, Dom Pedro, a young man of some twenty-three years, lieutenant to his majesty in the kingdom of Brazil, and then set sail for home. The general character of the Brazilian population had undergone a decided change since 1808. With Dom Juan had come a horde of needy adventurers, upon whom he had bestowed titles and lands. This had given rise to a new class, an aristocracy, who were looked upon first with distrust, then with hatred, by the native Brazilians.

After Dom Juan returned to Portugal the suspicions and fears of the Portuguese cortes were aroused concerning Brazil. This was owing partly because Dom Pedro was almost a Brazilian by education, and partly because of the revolutionary disturbances in some of the provinces, especially in Pernambuco and Bahia. As the Brazilian deputies were in the minority, the cortes were able to adopt a course of policy more and more opposed to Brazilian interests. They voted the suppression of superior courts of justice at Rio de Janeiro, they attempted to make the provinces depend directly upon Lisbon, and in a word they did their best to bring back the colonial system with all its worst faults.

. The final stroke was given when the cortes commanded Dom Pedro to return to Portugal. Nothing was better calculated to arouse the popular enthusiasm for him. The creoles rallied about him and implored him to remain in spite of the repeated commands from the cortes. Imperative dispatches were received by the prince when on the road near Sao Paolo on the 7th of September, 1822. He understood his position, and exclaiming, "Independencia ou morte!" struck the first blow of the revolution. His decision was received with the greatest enthusiasm, and on the 12th of October, 1822, he was proclaimed constitutional emperor and perpetual defender of Brazil. The Portuguese troops which were stationed here and there throughout the country made only a nominal resistance. The next great work was to organize a form of government. A popular assembly was called by the emperor in May, 1823, to which he addressed a message embodying most liberal ideas, as a basis for the proposed constitution. Unfortunately there were factious spirits in the assembly and nothing could be accomplished. The emperor dissolved the body and later in the year appointed a committee of ten who should formulate a constitution. This constitution was accepted by the emperor and by the authorities of the nation on the 25th of March, 1824, and was well received by the people. The popularity of the emperor was not of long duration. He seems never to have known how to become the man of the people, how to make himself entirely and truly a Brazilian. At the period of the revolution he had at times uttered sentiments calculated to encourage a spirit of nationality, and his sincerity had been credited; yet his subsequent employment of a foreign force, his continued interference in the affairs of Portugal, his institution of a secret cabinet, and his appointment of naturalized Portugese to the highest offices, to the apparent exclusion of the creoles, gave rise to the universal impression that the emperor himself was still a Portugese at heart. The native Brazilians grew restive under a government which seemed to be carried on in the interests of a foreign party. They accordingly broke out in open rebellion in many parts of the empire, and after several fruitless efforts at repression the emperor found himself in a painful and humiliating situation. On the 6th of April, 1831, the patriots held an assembly and demanded that a new ministry be formed. The emperor replied by assuring them that the administration was perfectly constitutional. But scarcely had the justice of the peace, who was commissioned to read the emperor's message, finished, than the document was torn from his hands and trampled under foot. The excitement increased, the ranks of the insurgents were reinforced, and finally the emperor was forced to submit. On the 7th of April he signed his abdication in favor of his son Dom Pedro de

Alcantara, a boy of six, and embarked for Portugal. The revolution of the 7th of April was not a local one, and it was not solely against an individual. It was a manifestation of the republican idea which before this time had shown itself in different states of Brazil. In Minas Geraes there had been an insurrection against monarchy in 1792. In 1801 there was a movement in Bahia, and in 1817 there was an organized revolution against the provincial government in Pernambuco. The leaders of the 7th of April were those men who believed it possible to have a constitutional government, with an emperor at the head who would obey their behests. For nine years the country was governed by a regency, and there was ample opportunity for the warring of factions. Some important constitutional changes were brought about in 1834. One of these created annual assemblies in the provinces, instead of the general councils before held. The members of these assemblies were to be elected once in two years. Another reform abolished the triple regency and conferred that office upon a single individual, to be elected every four years.

The year 1840 was signalized by a new and startling revolution, which resulted in the abolition of the regency. The emperor Dom Pedro II. was now in his fifteenth year, and the political party opposed to the regent and the existing ministry proposed to declare the emperor's minority expired and to place him in full possession on the throne. The constitution limited the minority at eighteen years, and the legislature had no power to amend or overstep the constitution. The debate upon the motion to declare the emperor of age began in the chamber of deputies early in July. At first it turned principally upon constitutional objections. The deputies grew excited, language became violent, the populace was aroused, and on the 23rd of July the regency was declared abolished.

As is nearly always the case, the very ones who were instrumental in helping Dom Pedro to declare himself master, failed to enjoy for any length of time the fruits of their devotion to the prince. Very soon he dismissed the liberal ministry and called into power the conservatives, without any other reason than his own good pleasure.

A monarchy was out of place in South America, surrounded as it was by republican governments, and itself not a natural growth but transplanted from another land. The present representative of the monarchical system did not by his conduct, during his long reign of more than fifty years, justify the claim of such a government to political existence. His policy, if it could be said that he had any, was a personal one. It consisted in ignoring men of true worth, and elevating those who knew how to be servile. The two parties, conservatives and liberals, to which belonged the politicians and statesmen, were called to office in turn at the caprice of the emperor. The natural result of this was, that men became unscrupulous, and had no party principles. His financial policy was marked by the same heedlessness of consequences. There was a constant deficit in the national accounts, and paper money was issued with a reckless disregard of its steady depreciation.

His attitude on the slave question alienated many of his subjects. Frequent movements were made during his reign towards the abolition of slavery, but he, in league with the planters, steadily opposed them. It was not until he was convinced by the stern logic of England's cannon that he agreed in 1871 to declare free all children of slaves.

He carried on various unreasonable and expensive wars against the neighboring republics. It would have been natural to suppose that a country as large and powerful as Brazil would have pursued the generous policy of protecting her weaker neighbors against the stronger. But the emperor never did this without imposing the most humiliating conditions. He considered the wars waged between the republics a pretext for diverting his own subjects from dwelling too much on internal affairs. He carried on a policy of centralization by forced constitutional changes, and false constitutional interpretations. The municipalities were deprived of their right to elect their own judicial and administrative officers. The provinces were robbed of all privileges which could arise from their provincial assemblies. The emperor appointed the presidents, secretaries, prefects of police, and the commanders of the provincial forces. In fact, the imperial system outrivalled in its rigidity and oppression the old colonial days. Dom Pedro was living a hundred years after his time, and with blind eyes failed to read the lessons of the republics about him. These faults in the imperial system, together with certain strong manifestations of the republican idea, brought about the fall of monarchy and established a new form of government.

About the year 1870 there began to be established throughout Brazil journals with a distinctly republican tone. This was especially true of the provincial journals, for they could exercise more freedom than those of the capital. A few of the more ardent spirits issued a manifesto, signed by their own names, in which they said: "We come before our countrymen with firmness and resolution, to lift the curtain from before the republican federative party. We are of America, we must be Americans." Before the revolution of 1889 there had been established seventy journals of avowed republican principle. They had a powerful influence in bringing about the revolution.

Another strong indication of republicanism was the abolition campaign of 1880. The emperor, as has been noted, signed an act in 1871 granting partial emancipation; but the provisions of the act had not been vigorously enforced, and the abuses of the system had continued. Voice was given to the movement by a deputy from the province of Sao Paolo, who introduced a bill in the chamber modifying the penal code. In his speech he exposed some of the cruelties that were practiced upon slaves in the plantations and the mines. The indignation of the deputies was aroused, and at their cry of righteous anger the country arose. Societies were organized, and propagandists went about preaching the doctrine of freedom to the oppressed. The campaign resulted in a complete victory for the abolitionists, and some of the leaders immediately sought to give a political significance to this enthusiasm for liberty which agitated the whole country.

Another fact that gave strength to the republican movement was that the heir to the throne, the emperor's daughter, was exceedingly unpopular. Fate seemed to conspire against a continuation of the monarchy.

Finally the army became disaffected, republican principles were freely discussed, and nearly all the younger officers became ardent republicans.

The revolution of the 15th of November, 1889, which gave to Brazil its present constitution, was thus the natural result of causes which had been at work for a century. Though long behind her sisters in declaring a republican form of government, she finally accomplished it by a bloodless revolution. On the morning of that day Benjamin Constant, who had been the leading republican thinker for the last five years, appeared by the side of General Deodoro da Fonseca at the head of several regiments. They marched to the place where the ministry was in session, and the national troops stationed there fraternized with them. They demanded the dissolution of the ministry, and the ministers immediately sent a communication to Petropolis, where the emperor was at that time, offering their resignations. The people took up the cry of "Long live the army, long live the Republic!" They met together in a popular assembly, and formulated an address to the army and navy: "We have the honor to inform you that after the noble and glorious resolution by which the monarchy has *ipso facto* been overturned, the people met together in the palace of the municipal council, in accordance with the laws yet in force, have declared complete the act abolishing the monarchy, and accordingly the youngest councillor, following the provisions of our laws, declares for Brazil a new form of government—the Republic. The undersigned hope that the patriots of the army will approve of the popular initiative by immediately decreeing this new republican form of government." The military leaders joined with the people, a provisional government was constituted with General Fonseca at the head, and the constitution of the United States of Brazil was framed.

II.

OUTLINE OF CONTENTS.

TITLE I.—OF THE FEDERAL ORGANIZATION.

SECTION I.—OF THE LEGISLATIVE AUTHORITY.

Chapter I.—General Dispositions.
Chapter II.—Of the Chamber.
Chapter III.—Of the Senate.
Chapter IV.—Of the Attributes of the Congress.
Chapter V.—Of Laws and Resolutions.

SECTION II.—OF THE EXECUTIVE POWERS.

Chapter I.—Of the President and Vice-President.
Chapter II.—Of the Election of President and Vice-President.
Chapter III.—Of the Attributes of the Executive Powers.
Chapter IV.—Of the Ministers of State.
Chapter V.—Of the Impeachment of the President.

SECTION III.—OF THE JUDICIAL POWERS.

TITLE II.—OF THE STATES.

TITLE III.—OF THE MUNICIPALITY.

TITLE IV.—OF BRAZILIAN CITIZENS.

SECTION I.—OF THE QUALIFICATIONS OF BRAZILIAN CITIZENS.

SECTION II.—DECLARATION OF RIGHTS.

TITLE V.—GENERAL PROVISIONS.

TEMPORARY PROVISIONS.

III.

CONSTITUTION OF THE UNITED STATES OF BRAZIL.

TITLE I.—OF THE FEDERAL ORGANIZATION.

ART. 1. The Brazilian nation adopting as a form of government the federative republic,[1] proclaimed by Decree No. 1, of November 15, 1889, constitutes itself, by a perpetual and indissoluble union between the former provinces, into the United States of Brazil.

ART. 2. Each of the former provinces will constitute a state, and the former neutral municipality will constitute the federal district, continuing to be the capital of the Union so long as congress shall not otherwise determine.

If congress shall resolve upon the removal of the capital, the territory having been chosen for this purpose, with the assent of the state or states from which it shall be dismembered, the present Federal District will by this act become a state.

ART. 3. The states may be mutually incorporated, be subdivided or dismembered, to be annexed to others, or to form new states, in accordance with the consent of the respective local legislatures for two consecutive years, and the approval of the National Congress.

ART. 4. To each state pertains the duty of providing, at its own expense, for the needs of its own government and administration, the Union having power to grant subsidies only in exceptional cases of public calamity.

[1] "The government is a monarchy, hereditary, constitutional and representative." Pol. Const. of the Empire of Brazil, Art. 3.

ART. 5. The Federal Government can not intervene in the nternal affairs of the state, except
  (1) To repel foreign invasion, or invasion from one state into another;
  (2) To maintain the republican federative form of government;
  (3) To re-establish order and tranquillity in the states upon requisition of the local authorities;
  (4) To insure the execution of laws of congress, and compliance with federal decrees.

ART. 6. It exclusively pertains to the Union to decree:
  (1) Taxes upon importations of foreign production;
  (2) Entry, clearance and port dues of ships; the coastwise commerce being free to domestic merchandise as well as to foreign upon which import duties have been already paid;
  (3) Stamp taxes;
  (4) Postal and telegraphic contributions;
  (5) The creation and maintenance of custom houses;
  (6) The establishment of banks of issue.
  The laws, acts and sentences of authorities of the Union will be executed throughout the country by federal officers.

ART. 7. It is prohibited to the Federal Government to create distinctions and preferences in favor of the ports of one state against those of the others by fiscal or commercial regulations.

ART. 8. It exclusively pertains to the state to decree taxes:
  (1) Upon the exportation of merchandise which shall not be from other states;
  (2) Upon landed property;
  (3) Upon the transfer of property.
  Sec. 1. The produce of other states is exempt from taxes in the state through which it passes for export.
  Sec. 2. From 1895 forward all duties on exportations will cease.
  Sec. 3. It is lawful for a state to tax the importation of

foreign merchandise only when it is destined for consumption in its own territory, the product of the tax, however, reverting to the federal treasury.

ART. 9. It is prohibited to the states to tax in any manner, or to embarass with whatsover obstacle or charge, legislative or administrative, the acts, institutions or services established by the government of the union.

ART. 10. It is prohibited to the states as well as the Union:
(1) To create taxes on the transit through the territory of the state, or in the passage from one to another, upon the products of other states of the Republic, or foreign countries, as well as upon the vehicles, of land or water, by which they are carried;
(2) To establish, aid or embarrass the exercise of religious worship;
(3) To enact retro-active laws.

ART. 11. In the questions which pertain concurrently to the government of the Union and the government of the states, the exercise of authority by the first will stay the action of the second, and annul thenceforward the laws and dispositions emanated therefrom.[2]

ART. 12. Beyond the sources of revenue specified in Arts. 6 and 8 it is lawful for the Union, as well as for the states, to create others not in contravention to Arts. 7, 9 and 19, Sec. 1.

ART. 13. The right of the Union and of the states to legislate upon railways and internal navigation will be regulated by a law of the National Congress.

ART. 14. The land and naval forces are permanent national institutions, destined to the defence of the country abroad and the maintenance of the laws at home. Within the limits of the

---

[2] The organization and administration of the provinces of the empire were essentially different from the methods of the republic. According to the imperial constitution the territory was divided into provinces, subject to re-division as the good of the state demanded, and provincial councils were held in a manner appointed by law, to propose, discuss and deliberate upon provincial affairs. It was forbidden them to propose or deliberate concerning the general welfare of the nation, concerning disputes between provinces, concerning taxes or the execution of the laws. The presidents of the provinces were appointed by the Emperor, and were removable when the interests of the state demanded it. Pol. Const. of the Empire of Brazil, Arts. 2, 72, 83 and 165.

law, the armed force is obedient each rank to its superior, and is obliged to sustain the constitutional institutions.

ART. 15. The legislative, executive and judicial authorities, harmonious and independent, correlatively, are organs of the national sovereignty.[3]

SECTION—I. OF THE LEGISLATIVE AUTHORITY.

CHAPTER I.—GENERAL DISPOSITIONS.

ART. 16. The legislative authority is exercised by the National Congress, with the sanction of the President of the Republic.

Sec. 1. The National Congress is composed of two branches: the Chamber of Deputies and the Senate.

Sec. 2. The elections for senators and deputies to the Chamber will be held simultaneously throughout the country.

Sec. 3. No one may be at the same time deputy and senator.

ART. 17. Congress will assemble at the federal capital upon May 3 every year, independent of convocation, and will remain in session for four months from the day of opening, the executive being empowered to prorogue or to call extraordinary sessions.

Sec. 1. Each legislature will be of three years' duration.[4]

Sec. 2. In the case of a vacancy occurring in congress the authorities of the respective states will immediately proceed to a new election.

---

[3] The departments of government recognized by the imperial constitution of Brazil were four: legislative, moderative, executive, and judicial. The moderative power was delegated to the Emperor, that "he may guard without ceasing the preservation of independence, the balance and harmony of the political powers." The moderative power was exercised in nominating senators from the triple lists, convoking extra sessions of the general assembly, sanctioning its resolutions, passing upon the resolutions of the provincial councils, appointing or removing ministers of state, in extending pardon to condemned criminals, and in declaring general amnesty. Pol. Const. of the Empire of Brazil, Arts. 10, 98, 101, clauses 1-9.

[4] The duration of the imperial legislature was four years. Pol. Const. of the Empire of Brazil, Art. 17.

ART. 18. The Chamber and Senate will meet separately, holding public sessions when the contrary may not be decided by the majority of votes present, and will only deliberate when there is present in each of the chambers an absolute majority of its members.

    Sec. 1. The rules of the two chambers will establish means for compelling absent members to appear.

    Sec. 2. Each of them will verify and confirm the powers of its members.

ART. 19. Each of the chambers will elect its officers, will organize its own rules, prescribing disciplinary penalties, including that of temporary suspension, for the respective members, will select its clerks, and will regulate its internal police service.

ART. 20. The deputies and senators cannot be held accountable for their opinions, words or votes in the exercise of their mandate.

ART. 21. The deputies and senators may not be arrested or prosecuted criminally, unless by order of their respective chamber, except *in flagrante delicto*. And in this case, the prosecution being carried to the point of indictment [*pronuncia exclusiva*], the prosecuting authority will remit the documents to the respective chamber for a decision as to relevancy of the accusation, should the accused not decide upon immediate sentence.

ART. 22. The members of the two chambers, upon taking their seats, will enter into a formal engagement, in open session, to fulfill their duties well.

ART. 23. During the sessions the senators and deputies will be entitled to a pecuniary compensation, beyond mileage, fixed by congress at the termination of each legislature for that to follow.[5]

ART. 24. Members of congress may not receive from the executive power remunerated employments or commissions, except they shall be diplomatic missions, military commissions, or offices of legal appointment or promotion.

---

[5] The compensation of deputies under the empire was the same, but that of senators was fixed at "one-half as much again as that received by the deputies." Pol. Const. of the Empire of Brazil, Arts. 39 and 51.

During legislative functions those of all others cease.[6]

ART. 25. The conditions of eligibility to the National Congress are :
(1) To be in possession of electoral rights ;
(2) To be a Brazilian citizen for over seven years in the case of the chamber, and for more than nine years in the case of the senate.[7]

ART. 26. The following are ineligible to the National Congress.
(1) The members of religious orders [*religiosos*] regular and secular, of whatever confession.
(2) Governors.
(3) Chiefs of Police.
(4) Commanders of garrisons, together with other military functionaries in command of land and naval forces equal or superior to these.
(5) Commanders of police corps.
(6) Magistrates, unless they have been unemployed for more than a year.
(7) Administrative employés who may be dismissed independent of process.[8]

[6] Senators and deputies could be nominated as ministers or councillors of state; in such a case the senator could retain his seat, but the deputy had to resign. However, in the case of the deputy a new election could be ordered, and if he were re-elected he could then hold both offices. Also, if when elected he exercised either the office of minister or of councillor of state he could combine both offices. All other offices were incompatible. Pol. Const. of the Empire of Brazil, Arts. 29, 30 and 32.

[7] No provision regarding length of time of citizenship was made in the imperial constitution.

[8] Under the imperial constitution those ineligible as deputies were, those not having a clear annual rental of at least $240.00, naturalized foreigners, and those not professing the state religion. Further qualifications were required for senators; they must be at least forty years of age, and must be persons "of wisdom, ability and bravery, preference being given to those who have served their country, and they must have an annual rent of at least $500.00." Pol. Const. of the Empire of Brazil, Arts. 45 and 95.

In addition to the foregoing general dispositions, the imperial constitution provided that members of both chambers should have the title of "August and Most Worthy Sir." Art. 16. It further provided that the emperor had no power to send any deputy or senator out of the country during sessions of the houses except in extraordinary cases, and then the respective houses were to be judges of the urgency of the case. Arts. 33 and 34. The imperial general assembly possessed other powers connected with the office of emperor, such as appointing a regent, recognizing the heir to the throne, appointing a tutor for the emperor if in his minority, etc. Art. 15 clauses 1-7.

CHAPTER II.—OF THE CHAMBER OF DEPUTIES.

ART. 27. The Chamber of Deputies is composed of the deputies from the federal district and those from the states in the proportion, which may not be reduced, of one for 70,000 inhabitants, and is elected by direct suffrage.

For this purpose the federal government will proceed within three years from the inauguration of the first congress, to a re-census of the population of the Republic, which will be revised every ten years.[9]

ART. 28. To the Chamber pertains the initiation of all tax laws, the fixing of land and naval forces, the discussion of projects submitted by the executive power and the declaration of the relevancy or irrelevancy of an accusation against the President of the Republic under the terms of Art. 52.[10]

CHAPTER III.—OF THE SENATE.

ART. 29. The senate is composed of citizens eligible under the conditions of Art. 25, chosen by the state legislatures by a plurality of votes to the number of three senators from each one.[11]

---

[9] The only provision made in the imperial constitution regarding the number of deputies is in Art. 97, which reads, "An organic law shall regulate elections and shall determine the number of deputies according to the population of the empire." No provision is made for the mandate except that it is limited (*temporal*). Art. 35.

[10] The imperial chamber of deputies had exclusive power to lay all taxes, to levy armies, and to name a new dynasty in case of the extinction of the reigning house. It also had power to hold a *residencia** of the previous administration, and to discuss acts proposed by the executive. As the person of the emperor was inviolable he was not subject to impeachment, but the chamber had the exclusive right to decree the impeachment of ministers and councillors of state. Pol. Const. of the Empire of Brazil, Arts. 36, 37, 38 and 99.

[11] Under the empire each province returned half as many senators as it had deputies. If the number chanced to be uneven in any province, it returned half the next lower even number. In the case of a province having but one deputy it could also return one senator. Senators and deputies were elected indirectly by the provinces. All active citizens voted for the provincial electors in the parochial assemblies, and these electors voted in turn for the provincial and national representatives. They voted for

*In the colonial days the viceroys and royal governors were subject to a *residencia* at the close of their term of office. The outgoing official was not permitted to leave the country for a certain length of time. During this time any one who had any complaint against the previous administration was given a hearing. The official had to answer such charges, and clear himself or suffer trial and punishment.

The senators from the federal district will be elected in the manner prescribed for the election of the President of the Republic.

ART. 30. The senator's mandate will continue for nine years, one-third of the senate to be renewed every three years.[12]

(1) In the first year of the first legislature, immediately after organization, the senate will divide its members into three equal groups whose mandates will end at the termination of the three triennial periods respectively.

(2) This division will be effected in the following manner: Three lists shall be made corresponding to the three groups. The first list shall contain the names of those senators who have received the highest number of votes in the states and in the federal district; the mandates of these senators shall be nine years. The second list shall contain the names of those who have received the next highest number of votes; the mandates of these senators shall expire at the end of the second triennial period. The third list shall contain the remainder of the names; the mandates of these senators shall expire at the end of the first triennial period.

(3) In case of a tie the oldest will be chosen, it being decided by lot in case of equality of age.

(4) The mandate of a senator elected to fill a vacancy shall continue to the end of the unexpired term.

ART. 31. The Vice-President of the Republic shall be *ipso facto* the president of the Senate, in which he shall have only a casting vote, and in case of his absence or disability his place will be taken by the vice-presidents of this chamber.[13]

ART. 32. It pertains especially to the senate to try the Pres-

the senators by triple lists, from which the emperor selected the ones having the majority of votes in all the lists together. Pol. Const. of the Empire of Brazil, Arts. 41, 43 and 90.

[12] Under the imperial constitution the senators were elected for life. The princes of the imperial house had a seat in the senate after they had reached the age of twenty-five years. Arts. 40 and 46.

[13] Under the empire the senate elected its own president. Pol. Const. of the Empire of Brazil, Art. 21.

ident of the Republic, and other federal functionaries designated by the constitution, in the manner and form by it prescribed.[14]

(1) The senate when deliberating as a tribunal of justice will be presided over by the president of the supreme Federal Tribunal.

(2) It will not pronounce a condemnatory sentence, unless two-thirds of the members be present.

(3) It may not impose penalties beyond the loss of office and prohibition from holding any other, without prejudice to the action of ordinary justice against the condemned party.

CHAPTER IV.—OF THE ATTRIBUTES OF CONGRESS.

ART. 33. It pertains especially to the National Congress.

(1) To estimate the revenue and fix the expenditure annually.

(2) To authorize the executive power power to contract loans and make other credit operations.

(3) To legislate as to the public debt, and establish means for its payment.

(4) To regulate the collection and distribution of the national revenues.

(5) To regulate international trade, as well as that between the states and the federal district, to create ports of entry, and to create and suppress bonded warehouses (*entrepots*).

(6) To legislate as to navigation on rivers that wash more than one state, or run through foreign territory.

(7) To decide the weight, value, inscription, standard and denomination of coins.

(8) To create banks of issue, legislate upon their currency and regulate it.

(9) To fix the standard of weights and measures.

---

[14] The imperial senate had exclusive judicial power in the case of transgressions committed by members of the imperial family, ministers of state, councillors of state, and senators, and also deputies during the period of the legislature. It had also certain other powers, such as convoking the assembly when the emperor failed to do so, or at the time of his death. Pol. Const. of the Empire of Brazil, Art. 47.

(10) Definitely to decide as to the limits of states between themselves, those of the Federal District and those of the national territory with adjoining countries.
(11) To decree the impeachment of the President of the Republic under the conditions of Art. 52.
(12) To authorize the government to declare war and to make peace.
(13) Definitely to decide as to treaties and conventions with foreign nations.
(14) To designate the capital of the Union.
(15) To concede subsidies to the states under the conditions of Art. 4.
(16) To legislate upon the service of post-offices and telegraphs.
(17) To adopt the necessary measures for the safety of the frontiers.
(18) To fix annually the land and naval forces.
(19) To regulate the composition of the army.
(20) To concede or refuse passage to foreign troops through the territory of the country for military operations.
(21) To call out and utilize the police force of the states in the cases provided for by the Constitution.
(22) To declare under martial law one or more localities of the national territory, in the emergency of attack by foreign troops, or domestic commotion, and to approve and suspend such declarations by the executive power or its responsible agents in the absence of congress.
(23) To regulate the conditions and process of election of federal officers throughout the country.
(24) To codify the civil, criminal and commercial laws of the Republic, and those of procedure.
(25) To fix the salaries of the ministers of state.
(26) To create and abolish federal public offices, to determine their powers, and to fix salaries.
(27) To constitute tribunals subordinate to the supreme federal tribunal.

(28) To legislate against piracy and offences against the laws of nations.
(29) To concede amnesty.
(30) To commute and pardon penalties imposed upon federal functionaries for crimes of responsibility.
(31) To legislate upon public lands and mines.
(32) To enact special laws for the federal district.
(33) To govern by special legislation those localities of the territory of the Republic needed for the establishment of arsenals or of other institutions for federal uses.
(34) To legislate upon higher instruction in the federal district.
(35) To regulate the cases of inter-state extradition.
(36) To be vigilant in the defence of the constitution and the laws, and to provide for necessities of a federal character.
(37) To decree the laws and resolutions needful for the exercise of the powers with which the constitution invests the government of the Union.
(38) To decree the organic laws for the complete execution of the constitution.

ART. 34. Congress is also charged, but not exclusively:
(1) To foster in the country the development of public education, agriculture, industry and immigration.
(2) To create institutions of higher and secondary education in the states.
(3) To promote primary and secondary education in the federal district.

Any other expenses whatsoever of a local character in the capital of the Republic shall be provided for exclusively by the municipal authority.[15]

---

[15] Many of the powers herein vested in congress were formerly vested in the emperor, either in his moderative or executive character. The powers indicated in Art. 33, Clauses 4, 12, 13, 19, 26, 29 and 30, were substantially vested in the Emperor. Pol. Const. of the Empire of Brazil; Art. 102, Clauses 13, 9, 8, 5, 4; Art. 101, Clauses 9 and 8.

CHAPTER V.—OF LAWS AND RESOLUTIONS.

Art. 35. All projects of laws may originate without distinction, observing the exceptions of Art. 28, in either the Senate or the Chamber, by the initiative of any of its members, or by proposal in a message from the executive power.

Art. 36. A project of law, passed by one of the chambers, will be submitted to the other; and the latter, if it be approved, will send it to the executive power, who, if he approves, shall sanction and promulgate it.

Sec. 1. If, however, the President of the Republic shall consider it unconstitutional or contrary to the interests of the nation, he must oppose it by his veto within ten working days from that upon which he received the project, returning it within the said time to the chamber wherein it originated, together with the reasons for refusal.

Sec. 2. The silence of the executive power upon the tenth day signifies a sanction, except in case the said period expires after the closing of Congress.

Sec. 3. The project being returned to the chamber wherein it originated, it will there be submitted to discussion and to a vote,* it being considered approved should it obtain two-thirds of the votes cast; and in this case it will be sent to the other chamber, whence, should it obtain the same majority, it will be returned as a law to the executive power for the formality of promulgation.

Sec. 4. Sanction and promulgation will be effected by these forms:

1. "The National Congress decrees, and I sanction the following law (or resolution)."
2. "The National Congress decrees and I promulgate the following law (or resolution)."

Art. 37. The project of a law of one chamber amended in another, will return to the first, which, should the amendment be accepted, will forward it, modified in conformity therewith, to the executive power.

* By calling the roll.

Sec. 1. In the contrary case, it will return to the amending chamber, where the alterations will only be considered approved if they obtain two-thirds of the votes cast; and in this case it will return to the originating chamber, which can only reject it by a two-thirds vote.

Sec. 2. If the amendment shall be rejected in this manner, the project will be sent to the executive for sanction without it.

ART. 38. Projects totally rejected or not sanctioned cannot be again proposed during the same legislative session.[16]

SECTION II.—OF THE EXECUTIVE POWER.

CHAPTER I.—OF THE PRESIDENT AND VICE-PRESIDENT.

ART. 39. The President of the United States of Brazil, as elective and supreme chief of the nation, exercises the executive power.

Sec. 1. The Vice-President elected at the same time with the President takes the place of the latter in case of temporary disability and succeeds him in case of vacancy.

---

[16] There are several points of difference regarding the enactment of laws under the republic and under the empire. Certain provisions were made in the case of the emperor introducing a bill, which he did by one of his ministers in the chamber of deputies. It was first examined by a committee from the chamber, and if approved by this committee, it was then admitted for discussion. The ministers of state were permitted to take part in the discussion, but had to withdraw when the bill was voted upon. If the bill introduced by the emperor failed to pass the chamber of deputies, he was informed of the fact in due form by a deputation. If it passed the chamber of deputies, it was sent to the senate. This form was also followed in the case of bills not introduced by the executive. At the second reading of the bill, if the originating chamber did not agree to the amendments made by the other chamber, it could, ar a meeting of the two houses, call for a committee of three members who should meet in the senate, and the dissenting chamber should abide by their decision. When a law had passed both chambers it was sent to the emperor by a deputation of seven members from the approving chamber. If the emperor disapproved of the bill, he expressed himself in the following terms: "The Emperor wishes to take time for deliberation upon the proposed law;" and the chamber answered: "We applaud the interest which your imperial majesty takes in the nation." This negative had only a suspensive effect, and if the two succeeding legislatures proposed the same bill in the same terms it passed over the emperor's veto and became a law. The time given the emperor in which to return a bill was one month. Pol. Const. of the Empire of Brazil, Arts. 52-70.

Sec. 2. In case of disqualification or vacancy in the office of vice-president, the vice-president of the senate, the president of the chamber of deputies, and the president of the supreme federal tribunal will be in succession called to the presidency.

Sec. 3. The qualifications for election as President or Vice-President of the Republic are:

(1) To be a native born Brazilian.
(2) To be in exercise of political rights.
(3) To be over 35 years of age.

ART. 40. The President will hold office for six years, and cannot be reëlected for the next presidential term.

Sec. 1. The Vice-President who assumes the presidency for three years of the presidential term, cannot be elected president for the next term.

Sec. 2. The president will lay aside the exercise of his functions without fail upon the same day upon which his presidential term expires, the president-elect to succeed him immediately.

Sec. 3. Should the latter be unable to serve or fail to appear, substitution must be made under the terms of the preceding article, Sections 1 and 2.

Sec. 4. The first presidential term will expire on November 15, 1896.

ART. 41. Upon assuming office the President will pronounce in the public session, before the supreme federal tribunal, this affirmation:

"I promise to maintain and execute with perfect loyalty the federal constitution, to promote the welfare of the Republic, to observe its laws, to sustain its union, integrity and independence." [17]

ART. 42. The President and Vice-President cannot leave

---

[17] The oath required of the emperor was: "I swear to uphold the Roman Catholic Apostolic religion and the integrity and indivisibility of the empire, to maintain and to cause to be maintained the political constitution of the Brazilian Nation, and all other laws of the empire, and to provide as far as in me lies, for the general welfare of Brazil." Pol. Const. of the Empire of Brazil, Art. 103.

the national territory without the permission of congress, under penalty of losing office.

ART. 43. The President and Vice-President will receive salaries fixed by congress in the preceding presidential term.[18]

CHAPTER II.—OF THE ELECTION OF PRESIDENT AND VICE-PRESIDENT.

ART. 44. The President and Vice-President will be chosen by the people by indirect election, for which purpose each state, as well as the federal district, will constitute a district with special electors, double in number that of the respective representation in congress.

Sec. 1. Beyond those specified in Art. 26, citizens who may occupy salaried offices, of legislative, administrative, judicial or military character, under the government of the Union, or those of the states, cannot be special electors.

Sec. 2. This election will be held on the 1st day of March of the last year of the presidential term.

ART. 45. On the 1st day of May following, the election of President and Vice-President will be held throughout the Republic.

Sec. 1. The electors of each state, as well as those of the federal district, will form a college, to meet together at the

---

[18] There are some interesting provisions regarding the imperial succession which it is appropriate to notice in this connection. The constitution declared Dom Pedro I. to be emperor, and his legitimate descendants to succeed him. The right of primogeniture was recognized, and in the same degree of kindred the preference was given to the male heirs. If the line were to die out, the general assembly were to name a new dynasty, with the condition that no foreigner could succeed to the throne. The emperor was considered a minor until he was twenty-eight years old; during his minority a regent ruled for him. This regent must be the nearest relative to the emperor in order of succession and must be twenty-five years old. If such a relative was not to be found, a regency was appointed by the general assembly, composed of three members. If at any time the emperor was incapable of exercising his office, the prince imperial was to govern for him, providing he was over twenty-eight years of age. If the heir presumptive to the throne was a woman, she could not marry without the consent of the emperor, or in case he was deceased, of the general assembly. Her husband was prohibited from taking part in the government, and could not enjoy the title of emperor until he had descendants by the empress. The allowances for the several members of the royal family were fixed by law. Pol. Const. of the Empire of Brazil, Arts. 105-130.

place which, with due notice, may be appointed by the respective governments.

Sec. 2. Each elector will vote by separate ballots for the president and for the vice-president. The candidates must be citizens, and one at least must be a native of another state.

Sec. 3. The votes being cast, two lists shall be made, containing the names of all candidates for the presidency and vice-presidency respectively. There shall be three copies of each list.

Sec. 4. The contents of these lists shall be made public immediately through the press. Two lists (one of each kind) shall be sent to the governor of the state, to be preserved in the state archives; in the federal district they shall be sent to the president of the municipality. Two lists shall be sent to the president of the senate, and the two remaining lists shall be sealed and preserved in the national archives.

Sec. 5. The two chambers being met in general assembly, the president of the senate presiding, he will open in their presence the two lists, and shall declare president and vice-president of the United States of Brazil the two citizens who in each list have received the absolute majority of votes.

Sec. 6. Should no one obtain this majority, congress will elect a President and Vice-President, by absolute majority, voting by call of names from among the three receiving the greatest number of votes in each one of the lists.

Sec. 7. In this election each state, as well as the federal district, shall have one vote; and this shall be given to that one of the three candidates who, in the respective representation in congress, shall receive a relative majority of votes.

Sec. 8. For this purpose the representatives of each state as well as those of the federal district, will vote by separate groups.

ART. 46. The general assembly for the verification of the election of President and Vice-President of the Republic will not be considered constituted unless there be present at least two-thirds of the members.

Sec. 1. The formality determined for this purpose by the

two preceding articles will commence and terminate at the same session.

Sec. 2. The roll of the members of congress being called, those present will not be permitted to withdraw from the house; for which purpose suitable measures shall be taken.

Sec. 3. No member present can abstain from voting.

CHAPTER III.—OF THE ATTRIBUTES OF THE EXECUTIVE POWER.

ART. 47. It pertains exclusively to the President of the Republic—

(1) To sanction, promulgate and make public the laws and resolutions of congress; to issue decrees, instructions and regulations for their faithful execution.

(2) To nominate and dismiss at pleasure the ministers of state.

(3) To exercise the supreme command of the land and naval forces of the United States of Brazil, as well as those of the local police, when called to arms in defence, external or internal, of the Union.

(4) To direct and distribute, under the laws of congress, according to the needs of the national government, the land and naval forces.

(5) To appoint to civil and military offices of a federal character, with the exception of the restrictions expressed in the constitution.

(6) To pardon and commute penalties for crimes subject to federal jurisdiction, except in the cases referred to in Art. 33, No. 30; and Art. 51, Sec. 2.

(7) To declare war and make peace under the conditions of Art. 33, No. 12.

(8) To declare war immediately in cases of invasion or of foreign aggression.

(9) To report annually upon the condition of the country to the national congress, recommending to it measures and urgent reforms, in a message which he will send to the secretary of the senate upon the opening day of the legislative session.

(10) To convoke congress for extraordinary sessions, and to prorogue its ordinary sessions.
(11) To nominate federal magistrates.
(12) To nominate the members of the supreme federal tribunal and diplomatic ministers, with the approval of the senate; it being permitted, in the absence of congress, to appoint them temporarily until the decision of the senate is pronounced.
(13) To nominate all other members of the diplomatic corps and the consular agents.
(14) To maintain relations with foreign states.
(15) To declare, by himself or his responsible agents, martial law in any locality of the national territory, in case of foreign aggression or serious internal disturbance (Arts. 77 and 33, No. 22).
(16) To open international negotiations, to make agreements, conventions and treaties, with the consent of congress; and to approve those made by the states, in conformity with Art. 64, submitting them, when necesary, to the authority of congress.[19]

CHAPTER IV.—OF THE MINISTERS OF STATE.

ART. 48. The President of the Republic is assisted by the ministers of state, agents of his confidence, who will sign their acts, and preside each at one of the departments into which which the federal administration shall be divided.[20]

---

[19] The powers of the emperor were more extensive than those accorded to the President. Besides possessing all the powers vested in the republican executive he could nominate senators from the triple lists; approve or negative the resolutions of the provincial councils, dissolve the Chamber of Deputies; remove as well as appoint judges; convoke the regular meeting of the new general assembly; appoint bishops and confer ecclesiastical benefices; remove as well as appoint all naval and military officers; enter into offensive and defensive alliances, reporting afterwards to Congress; declare war and make peace, reporting afterwards to Congress; grant papers of naturalization; grant titles, honors, and military orders. Pol. Const. of the Empire of Brazil; Art. 101, Clauses 1, 4, 5, and 7; Art. 102 Clauses 1, 2, 5, 8, 9, 10 and 11.

[20] Under the empire the number, office and times of meeting of the ministers of state were provided for by law. They confirmed or rejected the acts of the emperor, without which no act could be executed. Pol. Const. of Brazil. Arts. 131, 132.

ART. 49. The ministers of state cannot receive other employment or public functions, or be elected President or Vice-President of the Union.

ART. 50. The ministers of state cannot appear at the sessions of congress, and will communicate with it solely in writing, or personally in conferences with the committees of the chambers. The annual reports of the ministers will be addressed to the President of the Republic and by him communicated to congress.[21]

ART. 51. The ministers of state are not responsible to congress or to the supreme federal tribunal, for advice given the President of the Republic, except when such advice involves complicity with him in impeachable offences defined by the penal laws.

Sec. 1. They are responsible, however, for such acts as are held criminal by law.

Sec. 2. In impeachable crimes they will be prosecuted and judged by the supreme federal tribunal, and in those of complicity with the President of the Republic, by the authorities competent to judge the latter.[22]

[21] By the provisions of the imperial constitution, the ministers could take part in the discussion of a bill after it had been reported upon by the committee in the chamber of deputies, but they had to withdraw when a vote was taken. Pol. Const. of the Empire of Brazil, Art. 54.

[22] Under the empire the crimes for which a minister of state could be impeached were: treason, bribery or collusion, abuse of power, insubordination to law, acts against the liberty, security and property of citizens, misappropriation of public funds. The chamber of deputies had the exclusive right to impeach ministers of state, and they were tried by the senate. No foreigner, even if naturalized, could be a minister of state. Pol. Const. of the Empire of Brazil, Arts. 33, 38, 47 and 136.

The imperial constitution provided also for a council of state. The original provision was suppressed Aug. 12, 1834; but by the law of Nov. 23, 1841, a council of state was again created. According to this act the council of state was composed of twelve members, and as many substitutes, who met together with the ministers of state, the emperor presiding. The duties of this council were connected especially with the moderative power of the emperor. He was obliged to consult them and listen to their advice regarding declaration of war, negotiations with foreign powers, conflicts of jurisdiction between administrative powers, and between these and judicial powers, and abuses of ecclesiastical power.

CHAPTER V.—OF THE IMPEACHMENT OF THE PRESIDENT.[23]

ART. 52. The President of the United States of Brazil shall be liable to trial and judgment, after the chamber shall declare the indictment valid, before the supreme federal tribunal in case of common crimes, and before the senate in case of impeachment.

ART. 53. For the President of the Republic impeachable crimes are those which attack:
(1) The political existence of the Union.
(2) The constitution and the form of the federal government.
(3) The free exercise of political powers.
(4) The enjoyment and legal exercise of political or individual rights.
(5) The internal safety of the country.
(6) The integrity of the administration.
(7) The guardianship and constitutional employment of the public moneys.

Sec. 1. These offences will be defined in a special law.
Sec. 2. A second law will regulate the indictment, trial and judgment.
Sec. 3. Both of these laws shall be enacted in the first session of the first congress.

SECTION III.—OF THE JUDICIAL POWER.

ART. 54. The judicial power of the Union will have as organs a supreme federal tribunal, seated at the capital of the Republic, and as many federal judges and tribunals distributed throughout the country as congress shall create.

ART. 55. The supreme federal tribunal will be composed of fifteen judges appointed under the conditions of Art. 47, No. 11, from among the thirty senior federal judges and from citizens of notable wisdom and reputation, eligible to the senate.

---

[23] The emperor could not be impeached, as his person was held inviolable and sacred and he was not held responsible. But if for physical or moral causes he was rendered incapable of governing, and the majority of the general assembly so decreed, he could be removed and the prince imperial, if over twenty-eight years of age, reigned in his stead. Pol. Const. of the Empire of Brazil, Arts. 99 and 126.

Art. 56. The federal judges shall hold office for life, the position being forfeited only through judicial sentence.

Sec. 1. Their salaries shall be determined by a law of congress, which cannot reduce them.

Sec. 2. The senate shall judge the members of the supreme federal tribunal, and the latter the lower federal judges.

Art. 57. The federal tribunals will elect their presidents from their own membership, and will organize their respective clerical corps.

Sec. 1. In these offices, the appointment and dismissal of the respective employees, as well as the filling of the judicial offices in their ·respective judicial districts belong to the presidents of the said tribunals.

Sec. 2. The President of the Republic will designate from among the members of the supreme federal tribunal the attorney-general of the Republic, whose duties will be defined by law.[24]

Art. 58. To the supreme federal tribunal pertains:

I. To try and judge with original and exclusive jurisdiction:
 a) The President of the Republic in case of common crimes, and the ministers of state under the conditions of Art. 51.
 b) Diplomatic ministers in common crimes and in those of impeachment.

---

[24] The structure of the imperial judiciary was somewhat different. The constitution stated that the judicial power was independent, and was vested in judges and juries. It provided for a high court of justice to be composed of learned judges appointed for life from the courts of chancery in order of age. This court was established in the capital of the empire. It further provided that courts of chancery should be established in the provinces. These courts of chancery derived their name from the old Spanish courts of chancery which were replaced by the *audiencias* under the constitution of 1812. They were the courts of record and final resort in the provinces. In civil cases the parties were permitted to appoint arbitrating judges whose decisions were to be final. It was also decreed that no process whatever could be instituted unless conciliation had first been attempted; for this purpose there were justices of the peace elected in the same manner as were the members of the cabildos [This was determined by an organic law]. Pol. Const. of the Empire of Brazil, Arts. 151, 63, 153, 158, 160, 161 and 162.

c) Suits between the Union and the states, or between states.

d) Litigations and reclamations between foreign nations and the Union, or the states.

e) Conflicts of federal judges or tribunals among themselves, or between these and those of the states.

II. To try, on appeal, cases decided by the federal tribunal and judges, as well as those treated of in the present article, Sec. 1, and in Art. 60.

III. To review decided processes, under the terms of Art. 78 : Sec. 1. From sentences of the superior courts of the states there will be appeal to the supreme federal tribunal ;

a) When there is in dispute the validity or application of federal treaties and laws, and the decision of the state tribunal shall be contrary thereto.

b) When the validity of laws or acts of state governments is contested under the constitution or under federal laws, and the decision of the state tribunal shall consider valid the contested acts or laws.

Sec. 2. In cases in which state laws are to be applied, the federal court will observe the procedure of local tribunals ; and *vice versa*, state courts will observe the practice of federal tribunals when called upon to interpret laws of the Union.[25]

ART. 59. The federal judges and tribunals are empowered to decide :

a) Cases wherein either of the parties bases the complaint or the defence, upon a construction of the federal constitution.

b) Litigations between one state and the citizens of others, or between citizens of different states, under different laws.

---

[25] The jurisdiction of the imperial courts was not so closely defined. It belonged to the high court of justice to grant or deny new trials "in such cases and according to the form determined by law." It had original and exclusive jurisdiction in the case of official or unofficial crimes committed by its members, by officers of the courts of chancery, by officers of the diplomatic corps and by the president of the provinces. Also in investigation and decision of questions of jurisdiction and competency in the provincial courts of chancery. Pol. Const. of the Empire of Brazil, Art. 164.

c) Suits between foreign states and Brazilian citizens.

d) Suits brought by foreigners and based on contracts with the government of the Union, or upon conventions and treaties by the Union with other nations.

e) Questions of maritime and navigation law, both as to the high seas and to the rivers and lakes of the country.

f) Questions of international, civil and common law.

g) Political crimes.

Sec. 1. It is forbidden to congress to commit any federal jurisdiction to the state tribunals.

Sec. 2. Sentences and orders of federal magistrates will be executed by judicial officers of the Union, to whom, upon their requisition, the local police is obliged to render assistance.

ART. 60. Decisions of state judges or tribunals in cases to them pertaining, will be decisive in processes and suits, except as to

(1) *Habeas corpus*, or

(2) Effects of a foreigner deceased in cases not provided for by convention or treaty.

In such cases there will be an optional appeal to the supreme federal tribunal.

ART. 61. State courts may not intervene in questions submitted to the federal tribunals, or annul, amend or suspend their sentences or orders.

TITLE II.—OF THE STATES.

ART. 62. Each state will be governed by the constitution and laws by it adopted, provided that the organization must be under the republican form of government, must not be opposed to the constitutional principles of the Union, must respect the rights secured by this Constitution, and must observe the following rules :

(1) The executive, legislative and judicial authorities shall be separate and independent.

(2) The governors and members of the local legislature shall be elective.

(3) The judiciary shall not be elective.
(4) Judges may be dismissed from office only by sentence.
(5) Education will be secular and free in all grades, and gratuitous in the primary grade.[26]

ART. 63. A law of the National Congress will divide among the states a certain quantity of public lands, surveyed at their expense outside the zone of the frontiers of the Republic, with the condition of settling and colonizing them within a determined period, with reversion to the Union of the ceded land where this provision is not complied with.

The states may transfer these lands by any legal title, conditional or gratuitous, to individuals or associations which may propose to settle and colonize them.

ART. 64. It is permitted to the states;
(1) To make among themselves agreements and conventions of a non-political character. (Art. 47, No. 16).
(2) In general, all and every power, and right, which shall not be forbidden to them by an express prohibition of the constitution, or which shall be implicitly contained within the political organization by it established.[27]

[26] Chapter V. of Title IV. of the imperial constitution which referred to the provincial organization was amended Aug. 12, 1834. By its very minute and ample provisions the autonomy of the provinces was very much more limited than it is under the republican constitution. The governors, or presidents, as they were called, of the provinces were appointed by the emperor, and removed when the interests of the state demanded. The legislative power of a province was vested in a legislative assembly, the number of whose members was fixed in the constitution, *e. g.*, Pernambuco, Bahia, Rio Janeiro, Minas, Sao Paolo had thirty-six, Pará had twenty-eight, etc. The legislative assembly of any province had the right to petition to the national legislative power for the privilege of organizing a second chamber. The legislative assemblies were renewed every two years, the members being elected in the same way as the deputies to the national legislature. The legislative assemblies were granted the privilege of electing their own officers, and conducting their own affairs. They met annually for sessions of two months, the president of the province having the power to prorogue the assembly when he deemed it expedient. Pol. Const. of the Empire of Brazil; Law of the constitutional reforms of 1834.

[27] It was permitted the states, by the imperial constitution, to legislate regarding the civil, judicial and ecclesiastical division of the province, public instruction, provincial public works, navigation commerce, etc. There are twenty articles specifying the particular subjects pertaining to provincial legislation, all of which are of a particular

ART. 65. It is forbidden to the states:
(1) To refuse recognition to public documents of legislative, administrative, or judicial nature, of the Union or any of the states.
(2) To reject the money or bank issues in circulation by act of the federal government.
(3) To make or declare war one on the other, or to employ reprisals.
(4) To withhold the extradition of criminals demanded by courts of other states, or of the Federal District, according to the laws of Congress, by which this matter is governed (Art. 33, No. 35).

ART. 66. Excepting the restrictions specified in the constitution, and the rights of the respective municipality, the Federal District is directly governed by the federal authorities and exclusively subject to the tribunals of the Union.[28]

The Federal District will be organized by law of congress.

TITLE III.—OF THE MUNICIPALITY.

ART. 67. The states will be organized by their own laws, with respect to municipal government, upon the following basis:
(1) Autonomy of the municipality, in every respect, so far as regards their peculiar interests.
(2) Election of the local administration.

A law of congress will organize the municipality in the Federal District.

---

local character. Specific directions are also given for the enactment of provincia. laws. If the president of the province vetoed any bill which the legislative assembly had passed by a two-thirds vote, the bill could be sent to the national assembly for approval. If the national assembly was not in session at the time, it could be sent to the emperor, who had the power to order that it be executed provisionally until the national assembly should convene. Amendment of Aug. 12, 1834, to the Pol. Const. of the Empire of Brazil, Arts. 10, 11 and 14.

[28] Under the imperial constitution the provincial assemblies were forbidden to legislate regarding the general affairs of the nation; regarding conventions of one province with another; concerning taxes, the initiative of which lay with the chamber of deputies; concerning the execution of laws, retaining the right, nevertheless, of sending reasonable resolutions simultaneously to the general assembly and the executive power. Pol. Const. of the Empire of Brazil, Art. 83.

ART. 68. In municipal elections, resident foreigners will be electors, and eligible to office, in accordance with the conditions of a law to be prescribed by each state.[29]

TITLE IV.—OF BRAZILIAN CITIZENS.

SECTION I.—OF THE QUALIFICATIONS OF THE BRAZILIAN CITIZEN.

ART. 69. The following are Brazilian citizens:

(1) Those born in Brazil, even of a foreign father, he not being a resident in the service of his country.

(2) Son of a Brazilian father, and the illegitimate sons of a Brazilian mother, born in a foreign country, who shall become domiciled within the Republic.

(3) Sons of a Brazilian father who shall be in another country in the service of the Republic, notwithstanding they do not become domiciled.

(4) Foreigners who were present in Brazil on November 15, 1889, and shall not declare within six months after the Constitution shall become effective, their determination to preserve their original nationality.

(5) Foreigners holding real estate in Brazil, and married with Brazilian women, or having Brazilian sons, except they declare before the proper authority their intention to retain their nationality;

(6) Foreigners naturalized in whatsoever other manner.

Naturalization laws pertain exclusively to the federal legislative power.[30]

---

[29] The only provisions relating to municipal government under the empire were for the establishment of *cabildos* in every city or town which should be founded in the empire. These *cabildos* were the town council, consisting of members elected by the people. An organic law determined all things relating to municipal functions. Pol. Const. of the Empire of Brazil, Arts. 167, 168 and 169.

[30] The qualifications for Brazilian citizens set forth in the imperial constitution were virtually the same. Instead of the provision in clause 4 of the republican constitution, it stated that all natives of Portugal, or any of her possessions, who were residing in Brazil at the time when the provinces declared their independence, and who adhered to her, should have the rights of Brazilian citizenship. Pol. Const. of the Empire of Brazil, Art. 6, clause 4.

ART. 70. Citizens of 21 years of age are electors, who are registered in the terms of the law.

Sec. 1. The following can not be registered as electors for federal or for state elections :

(1) Paupers.
(2) Illiterate persons.
(3) Enlisted men, excepting the students of the military school of higher instruction.
(4) Members of monastical orders [*religiosos*], companies, congregations, or communities of whatsover denomination, subject to vows of obedience, rule or statute, which involves the renunciation of individual liberty.

Sec. 2. Elections for federal offices shall be regulated by law of Congress.

Sec. 3. Citizens not registered are ineligible.[31]

ART. 71. The rights of Brazilian citizenship may only be suspended or lost in the cases herein set forth :

Sec. 1. These rights are suspended :
a) By physical or moral incapacity.
b) By criminal conviction as long as this may remain in effect.

Sec. 2. They are lost :
a) By naturalization in a foreign country.

---

[31] Under the imperial constitution the voters in the primary elections [see note 11 p. 66] were "Brazilian citizens enjoying political rights," and all naturalized foreigners. Art. 91.

Those excluded from voting in the primary elections were :
1. All under 25 years of age, except married men, military officials of over 21 years of age, bachelors of arts, and clergy of the higher orders ;
2. Sons of families who reside with their parents unless they are engaged in the public profession ;
3. Menials and servants, except book-keepers, chief clerks in commercial houses, foremen of haciendas and factories ;
4. Members of monastical orders and all those who live in claustral communities ;
5. All those who have not an annual rent of $60.00.

All those qualified to vote in the primary elections were also eligible as electors for deputies, senators, and members of the provincial assemblies, with some additional qualifications. All voters in these elections must have a clear income of $120.00, they must not be defendants in suits of law, and they cannot be freedmen. Pol. Const. of the Empire of Brazil, Art. 92 and 94.

b) By the acceptance of foreign employment, pension, decoration or title without permission from the federal executive powers.

c) By judicial banishment.

Sec. 3. A federal law will provide the conditions for re acquiring the rights of a Brazilian citizen.

SECTION II.—DECLARATION OF RIGHTS.

ART. 72. The constitution assures to Brazilians and foreigners resident in the country, inviolabilty of rights relative to liberty, to individual safety, and to property under the following terms:

Sec. 1. No one can be obliged to do, or to leave undone, anything whatever except by virtue of the law.

Sec. 2. All are equal before the law. The Republic does not admit privileges of birth, disregards rights of nobility, does not create titles of rank, nor decorations.[32]

Sec. 3. All individuals and religious denominations may publicly and freely exercise their worship, associating themselves for this purpose, and acquiring property within the limits prescribed by the law of *mortmain*.[33]

Sec. 4. The Republic only recognizes civil marriage, which will always precede the religious ceremonies of whatever faith.

Sec. 5. Cemeteries shall be secular in character and administered by municipal authority.

Sec. 6. Instructions furnished by public institutions shall be secular.

Sec. 7. No denomination or church shall enjoy official aid, or hold relations of dependence or alliance with the government of the Union, or that of the States.

Sec. 8. The society of Jesuits is excluded from the

---

[32] The latter part of this clause was not in the imperial constitution, as a matter of course.

[33] Art. 5 of the imperial constitution establishes the Roman Catholic Apostolic faith as the religion of the empire; but it also provides that all other creeds shall be permitted to exercise their religion in houses designated for the purpose, but without any exterior churchly form.

country, and the founding of new convents or monastic orders is prohibited.[34]

Sec. 9. To all it is permitted to associate and unite together freely and without arms; the police cannot interfere except to maintain public order.

Sec. 10. It is permitted to everyone, whosoever it may be, to represent by means of petitions to the public authorities, to denounce to the authorities abuses, and to procure the indictment of culprits.

Sec. 11. In time of peace anyone may enter and leave the territory of the Republic with his fortune and property when and how he may choose independently of passport.

Sec. 12. The house is an inviolable asylum to the individual; no one may enter therein at night, without the consent of the dweller, except to succor victims of crimes and disasters, or during the day, except in the cases and in the manner by law prescribed.

Sec. 13. The expression of opinion is free on any subject, by the press or from the tribune, without subjection to censorship, each one being responsible for abuses in the cases and in the manner which the law shall prescribe.

Sec. 14. *Flagrante delicto* excepted, an arrest cannot be executed without a written order from the proper authority.

Sec. 15. No one may be detained in prison without specified charges save under the exceptions by law established, or imprisoned or detained therein, should he furnish satisfactory bail in cases where such is lawful.

Sec. 16 No one may be condemned except by the proper authority under an anterior law, and in the form prescribed by it.

Sec. 17. To the accused there will be secured by the law the fullest defence, with all resources and means essential thereto, beginning with the allegation of the crime [*nota de*

---

[34] Clauses 4, 5, 6, 7 and 8, referring to questions connected with religion, are peculiar to the republican constitution. These, together with clauses 21 and 22, which follow, are the only ones in this section which differ from the rights granted to the Brazilian citizen under the empire.

culpa], delivered in twenty-four hours to the prisoner, and signed by the authority, with the names of the plaintiff and witnesses.

Sec. 18. The right of property is maintained in all its plenitude, excepting disappropriation for necessity or public utility with previous indemnification.

Sec. 19. The seal of correspondence is inviolable.

Sec. 20. No penalty shall extend beyond the person of the delinquent.

Sec. 21. The punishment of the galleys is abolished.

Sec. 22. The death penalty for political crimes is also abolished.

Sec. 23. *Habeas corpus* will be granted whenever the individual may suffer violence or compulsion, through illegality or abuse of authority, or shall feel himself threatened by the evident imminence of this danger.

Sec. 24. With the exception of matters which from their nature pertain to special courts, there will be no privileged jurisdiction.

ART. 73. Public employment, civil and military, is open to all Brazilians, the conditions of special capacity prescribed by law being observed.

ART. 74. The officers of the army and navy will lose their commissions only by sentence passed in case of offences to which this penalty is attached.

ART. 75. The enumeration of the rights and guarantees expressed in the constitution does not exclude other guarantees and rights not enumerated, but which result from the form of government by it established and the principles contained therein.

TITLE V.—GENERAL PROVISIONS.

ART. 76. The citizen invested with functions in any one of the three departments cannot exercise those of another.

ART. 77. Any part of the territory of the Union may be declared under martial law, suspending therein the constitutional guarantees for a specified time, whenever the security of the

Republic demands this, in cases of foreign aggression or domestic violence (Art. 33, No. 22).

Sec. 1. Congress not being in session, and danger being imminent to the country, the federal executive power will exercise this attribute. (Art. 47, No. 15).

Sec. 2. During the period of martial law recourse to this will be restricted to measures of repression against persons:

(1) To detention in places not destined for common criminals.

(2) To banishment to other places in the national territory.

Sec. 3. Immediately upon the meeting of congress, the President of the Republic will report to it, with reasons, the exceptional measures to which he has resorted, the officers concerned being responsible for any abuse in the exercise of such extraordinary power.

ART. 78. Criminal proceedings decided may be revised at any time in the interests of the convicts by the supreme federal tribunal, to amend or confirm the sentence.

Sec. 1. The law will prescribe the cases and the form of the revision which may be required by the convict, by any one of the people, or *ex-officio* by the Attorney-General of the Republic.

Sec. 2. In the revision the penalties in the case reviewed cannot be increased.

ART. 79. Public functionaries are strictly responsible for abuses and omissions incurred in the exercise of their offices, as well as for indulgence or negligence in not effectively holding their subordinates responsible.

All officers will be bound by a formal engagement in the act of taking possession, for the fulfillment of their legal duties.

ART. 80. The laws of the former regime, while not revoked, will continue in vigor in what may not explicitly or by implication be contrary to the system of government established by this constitution, and to the principles therein consecrated.

ART. 81. The federal government guarantees the payment of the public, domestic and foreign debt.

ART. 82. Every Brazilian is bound to military service in defence of the country and the constitution, in accordance with the federal laws.

ART. 83. Military recruiting is abolished. The national army and navy will be formed by conscription, through a previous enrollment in which pecuniary exemption will not be admitted.

ART. 84. In no case directly or indirectly, alone or in alliance with another nation, will the United States of Brazil engage in a war of conquest.

ART. 85. The constitution may be amended through the initiative of the National Congress or of the legislatures of the states.

Sec. 1. A proposal of amendment will be considered when presented by at least a fourth part of the members of either of the chambers of the federal congress, and shall be passed in three discussions by a two-thirds vote of one and the other house of congress, or when it shall be requested by two-thirds of the states, each one represented by a majority of votes in the legislature, taken within the period of one year.

Sec. 2. This proposal will be considered approved if in the following year it shall be passed in the three discussions by a majority of three-fourths of the votes in the two chambers of congress.

Sec. 3. The proposal approved will be published with the signatures of the president and secretaries of the two chambers, becoming incorporated in the constitution as an integral part thereto.

Sec. 4. Bills tending to abolish the republican federative form of government, or the equality of representation in the senate, will not be admitted as subjects of deliberation in congress.[35]

---

[35] The imperial constitution provided that no amendment could be proposed until four years after its adoption. It could then be amended through the initiative of the chamber of deputies. Any proposition of amendment had to be made in writing and sustained by one-third of the members. The proposed amendment had to be read three times with an interval of six days between the successive readings. The

TEMPORARY PROVISIONS.

ARTICLE 1. Both of the Chambers of the first National Congress convoked for November 15, 1890, will be elected by direct popular election, according to the regulations decreed by the Provisional Government.

Section 1. This congress shall receive from the electoral body special powers to express the will of the nation upon this constitution, as well as to elect the first President and Vice-President of the Republic.

Sec. 2. When the first congress is assembled it will deliberate, in general assembly, the two chambers united, on this constitution, and, it being approved, it will proceed to elect, by an absolute majority of votes on the first ballot, and, if no one should receive this, by a relative majority (plurality) in the second, the President and Vice-President of the United States of Brazil.

Sec. 3. The President and Vice-President elected in accordance with the terms of the article, will occupy the presidency and vice-presidency of the Republic for the first presidential term.

Sec. 4. For this election there will be no disqualifications.

Sec. 5. This concluded, congress will consider its constituent mission terminated, and dividing into senate and chamber, will enter upon the exercise of its normal functions.

Sec. 6. For election to the first congress the disqualifications under the constitution, Art. 25, Nos. 2 to 7, will not be in force; but those excluded under this provision, once elected, will lose their offices, unless they declare their choice for the same as soon as they are recognized senators or deputies.

chamber then decided whether the bill should be admitted to discussion or not. If the necessity for constitutional reform was acknowledged by the chamber, and also by the senate, the emperor would then promulgate a law in the usual way, in which it was ordained that the electors of deputies to the following legislature should confer upon them special powers for effecting the proposed change. In the first session of the new legislature the amendment was discussed and passed upon in the usual way. Pol. Const. of the Empire of Brazil, Arts. 174, 175, 176, 177 and 178.

ART. 2. The acts of the provisional government, so far as they are not contrary to the constitution, shall be laws of the Republic until repealed by congress.

The commissions, posts and permanent appointments, concessions and contracts granted by the provisional government are guaranteed in all their plenitude.

ART. 3. The state which up to the end of 1892 shall not have made its constitution, will be subject, by act of the federal legislative power, to that of one of the others, which may appear most suitable for this purpose, until the state under this constitution shall amend it by the process in it prescribed.

ART. 4. In proportion as the states organize, the federal government will deliver to them the administration of the services which pertains to them under the constitution, and will then be released from responsibility for these services and for the payment of the respective staffs.

ART. 5. While the states are occupied in regulating expenses during the period of the organization of their services, the federal government, for this purpose, will grant to them special credits under conditions fixed by congress.

ART. 6. Within two years from the approval of the constitution by the first congress, the classification of revenue therein established shall become effective.

ART. 7. In the first appointments to the federal judgeships of the first and second instance, the president of the Republic will admit, as far as convenient to the proper selection of those tribunals and courts, the more important district and appellate judges [*juizes de direito e desembargadores*].

ART. 8. In the first organization of their respective courts the states will give preference, as far as the interest of the public service may permit, to the present judges of the first and second instance [*juizes de primeira e segunda instancia*].

ART. 9. The members of the supreme tribunal of justice not appointed to the supreme federal tribunal will be retired with full salary.

ART. 10. The *disembargadores* and *juizes de dereito*, who may under the new judiciary organization lose their positions, will receive their present salaries as long as they may be unemployed.

ART. 11. While the states are not constituted, the expenditure of the present magistracy will be for account of the federal treasury, but it will gradually be classified in proportion to the organization of the respective tribunals.

ART. 12. While the laws regulating military conscription are not perfectly organized, volunteers will be received in the land and naval forces.

We therefore order all authorities to whom the knowledge and execution of this decree pertains, to execute it, and to have it fully and exactly executed and observed.

The Minister of State for the Affairs of the Interior will have it printed, published, and made current.

Assembly-Room of the Provisional Government of the United States of Brazil, June 22, 1890, second of the Republic.

MANOEL DEODORO DA FONSECA.
RUY BARBOSA.
BENJAMIN CONSTANT BOTELHO DE MAGALHAES.
EDUARDO WANDENKOLK
FLORIANO PEIXOTO.
Q. BOCAYUVA.
M. FERRAZ DE CAMPOS SALLES.
JOSÉ CESARIO DE FARIA ALVIM
FRANCISCO GLYCERIO.

BIBLIOGRAPHY.

Arosemena; Constituciones Politicas.
Beauchamp; Histoire du Brésil.
Consular Reports, U. S.
D'Araujo; L'Idée Republicaine au Brésil.
Dictionaire de l'Economie.
Escriche: Diccionario de Legislacion.
London Times.
Southey; History of Brazil.
Winsor; Critical and Narrative History.

www.ingramcontent.com/pod-product-compliance
Lightning Source LLC
Chambersburg PA
CBHW031121160426
43192CB00008B/1067